THE COMMANDO FORCE

Britain's commandos were raised in World War Two in response to Prime Minister Winston Churchill's call for a force of "specially trained troops of the hunter class, who can develop a reign of terror down these coasts of occupied Europe, first of all on the butcher and bolt policy… leaving a trail of German corpses behind them."

Churchill's directive came after the fall of France in June 1940, and the British established a small, but well-trained and highly mobile, raiding and reconnaissance force drawn from volunteers across the Army and known as 'commandos'. Initially the force recruited from the British Army but soon came to welcome volunteers from several Allied nations as well as occupied territories. Following World War Two, the commando role transferred from the British Army to the Royal Marines, and the Royal Marines Commandos was born.

Today's commando force is fielded by the Royal Marines who maintain many of the high standards required to earn the coveted green beret that had been established by their forefathers. At 32 weeks, recruits to the commandos face the hardest and longest training of any infantry unit across NATO. It includes a timed 30-mile march across undulating terrain, a

nine-mile speed march carrying full equipment, an endurance course, and an aerial confidence test. But to reach those tests recruits must pass numerous challenges to prove their navigation, shooting and physical skills.

Once trained, a Royal Marine Commando can operate anywhere in the world from the blistering heat of the African desert, the humid atmosphere of the Brunei jungle, and in the inhospitable temperatures of the of the Arctic High North. The Commando Brigade includes frontline units who are specialists in mountain and arctic warfare, deploying maritime drug interdiction patrols in the Gulf, operating with partners to protect the Alliance's Northern Flank, while regularly training with US forces to maintain core skills, including jungle warfare.

Formed in 1664, the Royal Marines have evolved to become one of the most versatile forces in the UK military. Since World War Two, when the commando capability was raised, the Royal Marines have been on operations every year, with the exception of 1968. From Suez, where the commandos mounted the first helicopter assault, to Malaya, Aden, and Northern Ireland this elite corps has a colourful history which has shaped its reputation. They spearheaded the Falklands conflict, were constantly deployed in Iraq and

Afghanistan, and have more recently helped train Ukrainian marines. Today, the marine commandos are re-shaping their future in a project called Future Commando Force, which will see a focus on smaller, more highly skilled formations in which commandos use drones to navigate their way ashore to target an enemy. In the 21st century the commandos are training a force to deal with any crisis of the future. In one example of rapid intervention, marines from 40 Commando Royal Marines were deployed to Sudan in April 2023 to help oversee the evacuation of British nationals trapped in Khartoum when fighting erupted between government and rebel forces. Those who serve in this elite force are modest members of a unique club in which membership is only granted to those who have passed the gruelling selection course and won the right to wear the coveted green beret.

David Reynolds Editor

Royal Marine recruits wear a 'cap comforter' in the final stage of training to show they are about to undertake the commando tests. (DPL)

CONTENTS

44 The Post-War Years

At the end of World War Two, the Army Commando was disbanded, and the role assigned to the Royal Marines Commandos, who operated one brigade which included supporting Army units of Royal Engineers and the Royal Artillery. Within a couple of years conflict in the Far East would see the Royal Marines Commandos back in action in Korea where they assisted in the fighting withdrawal of a US Marine unit, then the green berets were into Suez, Malaya, and Aden.

54 The Falklands Conflict

On April 2, 1982 Argentinian troops invaded the Falklands, a small British dependency in the South Atlantic. A long-running claim by the South American country to sovereignty over the islands had finally erupted after General Leopoldo Galtieri was appointed President and announced that his administration would "undertake to recover 'the Malvinas', by military force if necessary."

66 Friends and Allies

The US Marines have had a long association with the Royal Marines Commandos. They served together in Korea, northern Iraq, the Balkans, and Afghanistan as well as training in jungle and arctic warfare. This close bond has resulted in many exchange drafts between the two corps. The Royal Marine Commandos have also developed close ties with their Dutch counterparts and their connections grown closer all the time.

78 The Longest War

When the first Royal Marine Commandos deployed to Northern Ireland in September 1969, few could have predicted that they would be the advance party for the corps' longest operational campaign and bear witness to some of the worst terrorist violence of the 20th century. Furthermore, no one could have forecast that more than three decades later the green berets would still be serving in the province until the peace initiative was finally secured.

88 The Commando Force

Commando operations inherently require a maritime force to allow them to mount operations and in the late 1990s a new dedicated helicopter carrier and an assault ship were seen as platforms that would allow the commando force to project power – as opposed to just deliver capability to an objective. This new concept saw a strong amphibious task force that could be at sea, ready to deploy a commando battlegroup to an area of conflict within hours or days.

The latest weapon in the commandos' arsenal is the KS-1 assault rifle. (MOD)

98 Afghanistan and Future Operations

Today's commando force has evolved to become a special maritime operations brigade capable of rapid intervention, hostage evacuation and poised to project military power with the deployment of littoral strike groups, in the high north and east of Suez capable of delivering combat readiness. In a new concept of operations termed the Future Commando Force, the marines are moving away from mass assaults across the beach and are focussed on small strike groups.

106 Commandos in 2045

The Commando Force of 2045 and beyond will be fully supported by digital technology and capable of delivering greater effect with smaller forces by adopting autonomous technology which can be integrated into the force. These unmanned platforms can provide medical evacuation, surveillance, air defence and direct mobile firepower generated from wheeled and tracked platforms as well as operating in the sub-surface and airborne environments. We look at the possibilities.

ISBN: 978 1 80282 973 0
Editor: David Reynolds
Senior editor, specials: Roger Mortimer
Email: roger.mortimer@keypublishing.com
Cover Design: Steve Donovan
Design: SJmagic DESIGN SERVICES, India
Advertising Sales Manager: Sam Clark
Email: sam.clark@keypublishing.com
Tel: 01780 755131
Advertising Production: Becky Antoniades
Email: Rebecca.antoniades@keypublishing.com

SUBSCRIPTION/MAIL ORDER
Key Publishing Ltd, PO Box 300, Stamford, Lincs, PE9 1NA
Tel: 01780 480404
Subscriptions email:
subs@keypublishing.com

Mail Order email: orders@keypublishing.com
Website: www.keypublishing.com/shop

PUBLISHING
Group CEO and Publisher: Adrian Cox
Published by
Key Publishing Ltd, PO Box 100, Stamford, Lincs, PE9 1XQ
Tel: 01780 755131
Website: www.keypublishing.com

PRINTING
Precision Colour Printing Ltd, Haldane, Halesfield 1, Telford, Shropshire. TF7 4QQ

DISTRIBUTION
Seymour Distribution Ltd, 2 Poultry Avenue, London, EC1A 9PU
Enquiries Line: 02074 294000.

BECOMING A ROYAL MARINES COMMANDO

Britain's Royal Marines Commandos are the UK's special maritime operations force held at high-readiness for operations across the globe. The men and women who apply to join do not do so for the money, this is an alternative career to the mainstream, packed with adventure and action. Within days of arriving at the Commando Training Centre recruits discover a new language of 'marine parlance' - the dining hall or restaurant is called the galley, food is known as scran, and doing something excellent is 'hoofing'. Rooms are 'grots', a drink is a wet and leaving the base is referred to as 'going ashore'. Finally, rookies are known as 'nods' – no doubt because they are permanently exhausted from the physical training and falling asleep.

To pass the commando training course you need to be physically and mentally robust as well as determined in the face of adversity with a desire to win at all costs. Success is all about an individual's 'will' not to give up. Those who serve in this elite corps become members of

Royal Marines Commandos are the UK's special maritime operations force held at high-readiness for operations across the globe and after training recruits can expect to be deployed within months. (MOD)

a unique club in which membership is only granted to those who have passed the gruelling selection course and won the privilege to wear the coveted green beret.

After the award of the green beret, the newly qualified Royal Marine Commando will be sent to a Commando unit and potentially be ready to operate anywhere across the globe from arctic Norway on the edge of NATO's northern flank to the deserts of Oman or Jordan. Today's Commando Force has been restructured to ensure the green berets have forces permanently at readiness in two-deployed groups, known as the Littoral Strike Groups. Based aboard Royal Navy support ships, one strike group of marines is assigned to the High North while a second sits in the eastern Mediterranean with the potential to move east of Suez. Their role is to provide an 'on call' force to evacuate British nationals trapped in areas of civil unrest, assist in a hostage rescue, or support humanitarian operations.

In one example of rapid intervention marines from 40 Commando deployed to Sudan in April 2023 to help oversee the evacuation of British nationals trapped in Khartoum when fighting erupted between government and rebel forces. ❯

In one example of rapid intervention, marines from 40 Commando deployed to Sudan in April 2023 to help oversee the evacuation of British nationals trapped in Khartoum when fighting erupted between government and rebel forces. (MOD)

Today's Commando Force has been restructured to ensure the green berets have forces permanently at readiness in two-deployed groups, known as the Littoral Strike Groups. (MOD)

Carrying all their newly issued equipment and assault rifle, the young trainees will quickly be introduced to living in the field on a nearby training area. (DPL)

Before trainees arrive at Lympstone, they are advised to get fit. But training in boots and wearing a heavy pack is not advised as you may cause injury before you arrive. (Jack Williams/DPL)

The Corps

The decision to join the Royal Marines – known to those serving, as 'the Corps' - is not one that should be taken lightly. Those who join will have a variety of reasons: some recruits have family connections, others travel thousand of miles from Commonwealth countries, increasingly others will have university degrees and view the marines as a challenge that they have always aspired to. The instructors are only interested in one fact, and that is the individuals' desire to pass at whatever cost.

Situated on the banks of the River Exe, just a few miles from Exmouth in Devon the base is officially known as the Commando Training Centre Royal Marines (CTCRM). It has its own railway station and new recruits must arrive by train at 'Lympstone Commando' - civilians cannot leave the train. The trainees are met on the platform by a corporal and escorted into the camp to the accommodation block which will be home for the first four weeks of training. Each recruit is allocated a bed and then off to the nearby barbers for a 'high and tight' haircut. By early evening these trainees - now part of a recruit troop - will be introduced to the base and receive a welcome from their company commander who will oversee their training. Rookies will then meet their training team and then make an oath to serve King and country in an attestation that enrols the new recruits into service. Unlike some armed forces units where there is no escape, recruits can decide throughout training that the Royal Marines is not for them and quit. Every day is a learning curve, the training team will deliver a healthy dose of banter to keep morale high and make sure that they spot anyone who looks like they are struggling and may need extra instruction.

Whatever an individual's reason for joining, if you have hopes of joining, preparation before your arrival at Lympstone is key. Make sure you run regularly, find somewhere to do pull-ups and carry out your own routine of press-ups and sit-ups every day. Training in boots and wearing a heavy pack is not advised as you may cause injury before you arrive. Don't over train, the physical training instructors have a tried and tested programme

Recruits will quickly be introduced to the various challenges including the regain tank which requires a rookie to crawl across a rope above a water tank, then drop his or her legs and then pull themselves up again-many end up in the water. (Jack Williams/DPL)

The first weeks of training will often see the trainees being put through their paces in the gym in the morning and attending lectures in the afternoon. (Jack Williams/DPL)

Recruits are issued with a Bergen, a back pack, and taught how to pack it and wear their combat equipment. (DPL)

which develops everyone to a standard that they can pass – providing recruits give 100%.

Applications can initially be made on-line or at recruitment centres in most UK towns and cities. After an interview the application process starts. For a young man or woman this is perhaps the most frustrating part of the journey to become a Royal Marine Commando. The system is managed by a civilian contractor and interviews, medical, and dental assessments as well as an eye test can take weeks, even months. You may also face a review of your NHS health record if you have suffered an injury or illness that

At the end of each major combat run naval medics will check the recruits' health. (Jack Williams/DPL)

Recruits will be taught how to rope down from a Royal Navy Merlin helicopter. (Patrick Allen/DPL)

Chemical warfare training involves recruits testing their respirator in the gas chamber. (Jack Williams/DPL)

or washed and ironed their own clothes. They will be issued with a Bergen, a back pack, and taught how to pack it and wear their combat equipment. The marines have a reputation across the armed forces for 'showering too much' and the importance of personal hygiene is highlighted so that recruits understand the relevance of keeping their body in good order to prevent problems in the jungle and other environments where perspiration can cause skin infections.

During these initial weeks, new arrivals wear a camouflage cap, so everyone knows they are in the ROP period of training. Success

the military deem requires more information. But don't be deterred by delays – if you are determined to get in you will. In almost all cases you will have support from the recruiting office and an Armed Forces Co-ordinator or AFCO. He or she will steer you through the process and keep in touch with you and eventually call you with a date to join.

Shock to the system

The first night at the camp is a shock to the system, recruits must be in bed for 10pm and lights out – a routine that many will not be used to. For some this will be their first time away from home, for a few it may be the first time they have made their own bed and not had permanent access to their phone. The following morning the Troop will be up early, marched to breakfast, then into the pool for an introduction to combat swimming, followed by a session in the gym and lectures in the afternoon. This phase is known as the Recruit Orientation Phase or ROP and is designed to prepare and physically condition recruits for Phase One training. These first weeks will often see the trainees on a routine of gym sessions in the morning and attending lectures in the afternoon.

Personal administration, such as locker inspections and making sure rookies have shaved correctly is important, as is being ready for duty on time. The ROP is a period in which instructors shape recruits to a standard that allows them to proceed into mainstream training. The cry 'Nod' can often be heard during training as an instructor seeks a volunteer for a task. Many 'Nods' have never worn boots, marched in a team,

Recruits will deploy on a nearby training area and undergo simulated night attacks and be taught how to use night-vision equipment. (Jack Williams/DPL)

Seaborne assault is a core skill which the recruits will use as they approach the end of their final commando training. (Jack Williams/DPL)

Cliff assault is a core skill for the rookie commandos who will learn how to scale cliffs and abseil back down. (MOD)

pace is hectic, and recruits are advised to focus on one day at a time. Rookies can also expect 'banter' from the Physical Training Instructors. This is not personal, the PTIs are the 'peacocks' of the training establishment and set the physical standard for the recruits to achieve. They will expect maximum effort from the trainees. Their task is to make sure that at the end of the ROP period trainees are now ready to start training. The PTIs are loud and shout instructions at recruits in a move to motivate and encourage them to work harder. Rookies must give 100% no matter how exhausted – and be ready to give more. At the end of the month-long ROP period recruits who passed the PT test will be awarded a blue beret at a small ceremony and move accommodation ready to begin Phase One training.

Phase One Training

Mike Johnson, who joined the marines in 2001, remembers his first few days at Lympstone. He said: "I don't think we had a foundation period then; we just went straight into training and I didn't know what had hit me. We were marched away for haircuts and were issued with a uniform. It is difficult to describe how I felt, but I think we were all anxious preparing for the next day, making sure all your kit is ready and thinking about the day ahead. Unless you have actually been there and done it, I am not sure that you can appreciate it. The physical training is a major culture shock. I never knew I could run so far and I think on reflection it was the prospect of running with all the kit that really worried me. I'll be honest, it was the best decision of my life, the training, culture, and ➲

in Foundation and throughout training at Lympstone is all about being organised and making sure you know what you are doing and when. Each night instructors will post 'daily orders' for the following day. Mornings start very early with breakfast at 6am and recruits will need to shower, make their bed, clean the toilets and make sure their locker is ready for a potential inspection. These checks are designed to make sure individuals can organise themselves and keep their equipment and clothing clean.

In these first weeks recruits will be expected to learn some facts about the Corps: when was it formed, how many Victoria Crosses have been awarded, and who is the captain general? The

At some point recruits will use the fast armoured assault craft which are likely to be introduced in their final test exercise. (MOD)

Much of the physical training involves being able to carry heavy weights over long distance which will be required when the trained commandos get to their units. (MOD)

The Armoured Support Group provides tracked personnel carriers which the recruits will learn how to drive at the end of training. (MOD)

exercise at Gutter Tor on Dartmoor, listed in the *Guinness Book of Records* for the most changes of inclement weather in an hour. He said: "The training team told us that food was on the way. Sure enough, a lorry arrived with a number of green boxes, we called 'hay boxes'. We all lined up and I remember thinking that there was a lot of boxes. We were told to open them and a live chicken jumped out – that was our dinner! We had been taught how to cook food in earth ovens weeks before and now we had to put that knowledge to good use. That was a challenge."

For many years Phase One training was held at Deal in Kent. Here recruits faced what many called 'old school' training that would be unacceptable today. Rob Watson served at Deal and recalls the training was harsh but fair. He said: "I arrived at Deal on a cold and wet September afternoon in the late 1970s having caught the train from London. I hadn't got a clue

brotherhood that I experienced shaped me for life and while I only served four years I would do it all again, it was brilliant."

Phase One training starts with a bang as the rookies are back in the gym climbing ropes, deployed on exercises, and being put through their paces on the assault course – otherwise known as 'bottom-field'. As training progresses recruits will find themselves on the range, map reading, and battling their way through a mock house complex in procedure known as 'close quarter battle'. Adverts for the Royal Marines proclaim that being a marine is all about a 'state of mind' and that could not be more relevant when it comes to some of the basic tests the recruits face. In one exercise trainees will be expected to wade through chest deep water wearing full combat clothing and equipment in darkness. It is slightly uncomfortable but not hard, yet some struggle as the brain sees cold deep water as an impossible challenge. Overcoming the cold is all in the mind. They will face endurance marches, known as yomps, navigation tests and more and more exercises in areas such as Salisbury Plain.

In the early weeks of training recruits find themselves on Dartmoor in what is essentially a survival exercise. Carrying all their newly issued equipment and assault rifle the young trainees will yomp across the moor and in the late afternoon make themselves a shelter prior to a survival exercise. Jim Berry who went through training in the 1980s remember his survival

The majority of recruit exercises are held at night when navigation tests will be conducted. (MOD)

Recruits will be issued with night-vision goggles and learn to use them during night marches. (MOD)

All recruits will be required to pass a close quarter battle test in which teams rescue a hostage without shooting the good guys! (MOD).

staying awake while on sentry duty. Many, if not all recruits, will fall asleep at least once which risks being caught by the training team and if they don't wake up their rifle could be confiscated. Week after week recruits will climb the 30ft ropes and race around the assault course – then carry a colleague in a fireman's lift over a set distance.

PTIs will teach the recruits how to approach each task, reaching the top of the ropes requires technique as does the assault course, but all need personal determination and aggression. The culmination of Phase One Training peaks with a series of tests to ensure each recruit is ready to pass into Phase Two. At the same time as recruits progress through training young officers undergo the same training and several times a year personnel from across the British Army attend the All-Arms Commando Course – these are usually people who are due to be attached to the Commando Brigade. As recruits move into Phase Two, they will have developed confidence in their physical ability and knowledge to face the challenges ahead of them which will culminate in the commando tests. ●

what to expect, although I had read just about every leaflet I could about the Marines. The train was full of lads and we all looked each other up and down. When we arrived at Deal it was obvious we were heading for the same place as we hung around outside the station. A navy-blue coach pitched up with Royal Marines in big white letters stamped across the side. A small, tough looking corporal walked across to us with a clipboard and ticked our names off as we climbed aboard the vehicle. A few minutes drive and we were in Deal barracks."

As Phase One at CTCRM continues recruits are expected to keep their SA80 assault rifle immaculate at all times and always on their person. Rookies are taught how to live and fight in the field making sure they never leave any equipment behind which could give their position away to the enemy. When deployed on a nearby training area rookies will undergo simulated night attacks and be taught to use night-vision equipment. One of the most difficult tasks is

As training ramps up, recruits will use radios, be expected to map read on their own and plan section attacks. (MOD)

A week of field firing will involve learning how to operate the NLAW antitank weapon. (MOD)

The training of today's recruits maintains the level of excellence that has produced commandos since the formation of the role in World War Two, with a selection process that is the longest of any infantry unit in Europe. (MOD)

'STATE OF MIND'

The training of today's recruits maintains the same levels of excellence that has produced commandos since the creation of the role in World War Two, with a selection process that is the longest of any infantry unit in Europe. The mantra of this green beret force is often repeated by recruiting officers: "We're not your typical soldier. We've got something others haven't. The bit sitting under the green beret that lets us power on when others would quit, and get the job done, even when the odds aren't in our favour. You're not born with it, but you can develop it. It's a state of mind".

It is this self-belief and confidence in their own ability that is instilled in recruits and will allow them to overcome and succeed. While the standard of the commando tests remains exactly the same today as they have always been, the training programme has been adjusted to meet the demands of today's Royal Marines. As the UK's armed forces evolve to meet changing and challenging global demands the marines have launched a new concept, called the Future Commando Force designed to shape the Royal Marines into an expeditionary raiding force. It has been adopted as the days of troops charging across enemy held beaches are clearly over and modern weapon systems can hit ships hundreds of miles out from an objective. To respond to this the commandos are moving towards strike groups which can deploy independently or in support of other forces. As a consequence, the marines need every man in a strike group to be an expert map reader, marksman, drone operator, and an authority in close quarter battle as well as being potentially able to use artificial intelligence. These skill sets have been added to training and without question, today's recruits are trained to a very high standard.

Second Phase Training

The second phase of training at the Commando Training Centre Royal Marines

Royal Marines build self-belief and confidence in their own ability that will allow them to overcome and later deploy on operations in areas such as Afghanistan. (MOD)

(CTCRM) – the serious business of working towards the 'green beret' - starts at a faster pace than their early weeks with recruits now given more responsibility and expected to plan and prepare for training exercises. The Lympstone base enjoys some of the best facilities in the armed forces with its own modern gymnasium, swimming pool, and complex of outdoor assault courses – it is a mecca of military physical fitness. On average, 1,300 recruits, 2,000 potential recruits and 400 potential officers attend training courses and acquaintance courses every year. Military tactics and training now ramp up as recruits are trained to undertake the classic commando skills of cliff assault, abseiling, roping down from helicopters and mounting night raids. Recruits also face an increase in the tempo of combat fitness – this involves runs carrying rifle and full equipment, an introduction to the 'Tarzan course' and the the endurance course as well as the 'regain tank' – here recruits must pull themselves across a rope over a water tank then hold on within their hands, drop their legs and then pull themselves back up. This process is called a regain and it can often end up with the rookie going into the water.

Phase two leaves the gym behind, all physical training is now in boots and recruits progress

Phase two of a Marine Commando's training sees the recruits working towards the final stages of the process and the tests to earn the green beret. (MOD)

Recruits will need to operate in a strike group and to be an expert map reader, marksman, and drone operator. (MOD)

to learning skills that include operating in small teams to collate reconnaissance and surveillance, tactical navigation, and communications as well as specialist medical training. The trainee will learn to handle and fire all the infantry weapons systems that he or she will carry as well as the support systems they may be expected to use in a commando unit. From learning about and using the L109A1 grenade, the SA80 and underslung grenade launcher, to the Glock pistol and General-Purpose Machine Gun (GPMG) and N-LAW anti-tank weapon. In addition, the marines have adopted a new rifle, the Knights Stoner 1 (KS-1) designated the L403A1.

Training culminates in a final exercise in which the recruits face days of night patrolling, followed by a series of endurance marches. After several days in the field the troop is airlifted by helicopter and flown to an assault ship. Here the troop is given a target to assault and orders to free a hostage being held at a coastal fort. After a briefing and final preparation, the troop now splits into strike groups and embarks in fast assault craft. In darkness they'll head for a beach where an advance force is already waiting to lead them ashore. Here they mount a cliff assault and then spend a day observing the target and

Trainees will now face regular speed marches to prepare them for the commando tests. (Jack Williams/DPL)

carrying out close reconnaissance. Twelve hours later they move through the dead of night, one group tasked to carry out a deception operation while the remaining strike teams engage the rebel force and rescue the hostage.

At this stage of training the Tarzan course, the nine-mile speed march, and the endurance course will be familiar to the troop – after weeks of rehearsals. The one exception is the 30-miler which recruits will have heard about but will not have any experience of.

The nine-mile speed march is the first test. It needs to be completed in 90 minutes, as a squad, while carrying 30lb of equipment and rifle. At the start-line instructors check the weight of each person's equipment, any whose equipment is underweight will have their webbing topped up with rocks. Some recruits will wear their lucky socks – ones they had used for test events throughout training. Others will follow the same routine of breakfast and plenty of water in order to keep calm. Once the runs start the speed carries the troop forward with the only stops being for water. Recruits must give everything in mind and body or face defeat, often in Heartbreak Lane, an infamous landmark which forms the finishing mile of most runs. At the end of all combat runs , in which recruits carry ➲

Recruits learn to handle and fire all the infantry weapons systems used in a commando unit as well as the anti-tank systems. (Jack Williams/DPL)

In stage two of their training recruits also face an increase in the tempo of combat fitness (MOD)

Helicopters are often used to ferry the recruits on exercises. (MOD)

The endurance course is an intense two- miles of tunnels, pools, streams, bogs, and woods. Here rookies face the sheep dip or water tunnel which has become legend within Lympstone. Recruits hear stories of rookies getting stuck, but the reality is that instructors are there to ensure safety. As trainees finish the endurance course, they face a four-mile run back to camp where recruits will then need to fire their weapons and need to score six hits on a target.

For the final test, recruits are bussed to Okehampton battle camp – an isolated wartime camp on Dartmoor. After a few

equipment and rifles, recruits are halted outside the camp and their physical condition checked before they cross the road bridge and march back into camp. Once back in camp, staff and instructors line the main road to congratulate the troop as they march into the base headed by two Royal Marine drummers. The first event is finished, three to go.

Confidence Course

The Tarzan course is an aerial confidence course which needs to be completed in 13 minutes, while carrying 30lb of equipment and rifle. Again, some recruits carry out their routines, then after their equipment is weighed the event starts. Rookies climb a tower and launch themselves off a Tarzan slide then race across obstacles fixed high in the tress and on the ground. The final challenge is a 30ft wall which the recruits must pull themselves up on a rope.

Recruits must be able to abseil down a cliff face at speed. (Patrick Allen/DPL)

The 'regain tank' — here recruits must pull themselves across a rope over a water tank then hold on with their hands, drop their legs, and then pull themselves back up. (MOD)

More cliff assault training is now introduced to the commando course. (Jack Williams/DPL)

The assault course on the bottom field of the training area includes more than a dozen obstacles. (Jack Williams/DPL)

The 30ft ropes — success here is all about using the technique that the instructors teach recruits. (MOD)

The Tarzan course is an aerial confidence exercise which needs to be completed in 13 minutes, while carrying 30lb of equipment and a rifle. (Jack Williams/DPL)

The recruits face a race against the clock as they tackle a series of challenges high off the ground. (Jack Williams/DPL)

On the endurance course recruits plough through a water obstacle called Peter's pool as they start the event (MOD)

hours sleep the rookies are up at 4am for breakfast and an early start on the 30-mile march. This is an endurance march across Dartmoor, which needs to be completed in less than eight hours, carrying 40lb of equipment and a rifle. For some the weather is bright and sunny, others face fog and driving rain or snow and ice which makes the yomp more challenging. Once they finish at the barracks of 42 Commando on the edge of Dartmoor, they parade in front of their commanding officer and are presented with their green berets- they are now trained ranks. The troop are now the King's Squad and spend the following week on the parade square preparing for their pass-out parade. The 'Kings Squad' is the culmination of 32 weeks Royal Marines Commando training and a tradition that has been in place since King George V granted the honour in 1918.

Rookies climb a tower and launch themselves off a Tarzan slide then race across obstacles fixed high in the trees as well as on the ground. (MOD)

During the series of tunnels and tubes they must pass though the sheep dip, a submerged tunnel full of water. (Jack Williams/DPL)

During the recent Afghanistan operations, recruits were often sent on operations to Helmand within weeks of completing their training. (MOD).

Within weeks, some recruits will be in commando units and potentially deployed anywhere in the world. (MOD)

Officer Training

Royal Marines Commando Officer Initial Training is one of the longest and most arduous programmes in the world. You'll need to be in the best condition of your life to make it through. Lasting 16 months, your training will cover everything you need to learn, develop, hone and master to be able to do everything you might ask of your team. You'll also be trained in advanced tactical and command skills. If

A week after the 30 miler recruits will pass out at a parade called the King's Squad. (MOD)

you're successful, you'll have a base level of fitness that will benefit you as you start your career. There are five phases to training, most of which have physical elements and all of which are challenging, testing and demanding. You will be tested at every stage and, once trained to a suitable a level, expected to complete two

The run back to camp after the endurance course demands determination. (Jack Williams/DPL)

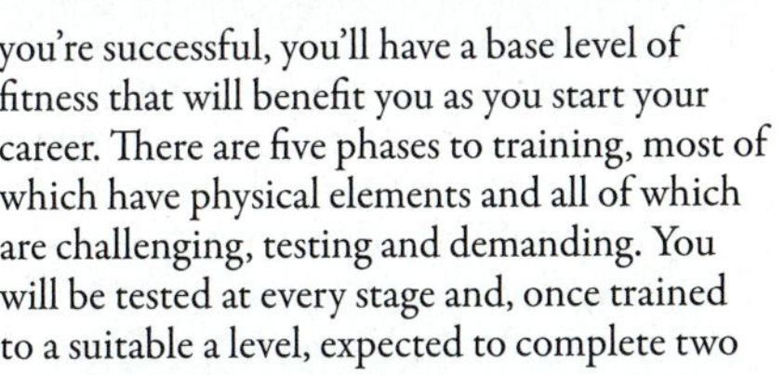

The 30 miler is the final event of training and at the end recruits are presented with their green berets. (MOD).

specific challenges to prove you have the mettle and state of mind to be a Royal Marines officer.

On leaving Lympstone, a newly qualified marine or officer can be sent to an operational unit. The in-depth training he receives at Lympstone will always remain with him as a bedrock of his character, even after he has left the corps. A small but powerful force, the Royal Marines have served in some capacity in every military operation since World War Two and deployed on active service every year, except 1968. The green beret has been worn by generations of successful recruits who will tell you that their famous headgear comes in just one size - proud. ●

FORMATION
THE ARMY COMMANDOS

The formation of the Army Commandos in 1940 called for a special breed of soldier to volunteer for a new concept in warfare that could not afford to fail. In mid-1940 the Prime Minister Winston Churchill called for a new force to be created to carry out amphibious raids on enemy territory. He said: "Enterprises must be prepared, with specially-trained troops of the hunter class, who can develop a reign of terror down these coasts, first of all on the 'butcher and bolt', policy." His call came after the Germans had trapped the British Expeditionary Force (BEF) in France and forced it to withdraw to Dunkirk. Britain faced its 'darkest hour' and desperately needed a force to strike back at the Nazis who had inflicted so much damage. In Whitehall, a study of irregular warfare had been made in the late 1930s by two officers assigned to a small research team within the War Office. Lieutenant Colonel John Holland, a Royal Engineer officer, and Major Colin Gubbins of the Royal Artillery had identified the success of the Boers, who deployed small units of men and ignored the contemporary principles of conventional warfare. They mounted surprise hit-and-run raids. The concept was adopted by the War Office and the British Army rose to the challenge. Volunteers quickly stepped forward and formed ten Commando (Cdo) units. In early 1941 Operation Claymore was mounted by Nos 3 and 4 Cdo and successfully destroyed German resources in the Norwegian Lofoten islands, including petrol dumps and capturing encrypted equipment and codebooks.

Commando operations were now being planed and executed at pace, in France, Norway,

During World War Two, army volunteers trained at Achnacarry in Scotland and were then posted to their relevant commando units before taking part in raids in Norway and France. (DPL)

The commando role was passed to the Royal Marines at the end of World War Two , but a small number of army personnel continue to serve with today's commando force. (MOD)

Libya and beyond. In December, 1941 there were two raids in Norway. The first, which took place on December 26, was Operation Anklet - a raid on the Loften Islands by No. 12 Cdo. This provided a diversion for a larger attack at Vagsoy island, called Operation Archery. The objectives of both were quickly achieved, and the forces re-embarked after two days. The second raid on December 27, Operation Archery, involved men from Nos. 2, 3, 4 and 6 Cdos. The raid caused significant damage to factories, warehouses, the German garrison, and also sank eight ships.

In early 1941 Lord Louis Mountbatten was commanding the destroyer HMS *Kelly* and in August of the same year he was appointed captain of the aircraft carrier HMS *Illustrious* which lay in Norfolk, Virginia, for repairs following action at Malta. On his way to join the carrier in the United States, Prime Minister Winston Churchill recalled him to the UK and in October appointed him Chief of Combined Operations this was a new position, replacing the former Director of Combined Operations Admiral Sir Roger Keyes, and giving Mountbatten a wider operational remit. After a two-month working handover Lord Mountbatten assumed the post in early 1942.

Lord Mountbatten was keen to promote the commando capability and saw the strategically important German dry dock base at St Nazaire as a priority. This massive installation was used as the maintenance and repair stop for Germany's powerful battleships, including the *Tirpitz*, and the battle cruisers *Scharnhorst* and *Gneisenau*. In February 1942, Lieutenant Colonel Augustus Charles Newman was selected to command and plan the raid, codenamed Operation Chariot. The Germans believed St Nazaire was secure from assault and considered any plan to attack it as 'suicidal'. However, Combined Operations listed the dry dock as the prime target. HMS *Campbeltown*, a former US Navy destroyer, was key to the plan. The warship was stripped inside of all equipment to reduce her weight and draught in the water and packed with explosives. The plan was for the vessel to ram the dry-dock gates then the explosives in her hull would be ignited later.

The explosive charges were fitted with timing devices designed to detonate hours after the ship rammed the dock gates - the commandos and sailors would by then have abandoned the vessel. Late on March 27, the force, headed by HMS *Campbeltown* with 18 gunboats in support, all packed with commandos, sailed into the Loire estuary. The profile of the 50-year-old warship had been altered to make her look like a German vessel.

Snipers, although they have newer weapons and equipment, adopt the same principles of fieldcraft used by commando snipers in World War Two. (Guy Channing/DPL)

She also flew the German ensign. As the ship approached the port in darkness she came under intense fire, but against all odds made it to the dry-dock gates.

The destroyer rammed the dry-dock gates at 0134hrs on March 28. As the fighting ended the Germans boarded the warship to search for more commandos, believing the raid was over. Then, at 1035hrs in the morning light the explosives ignited. More than 400 Germans died in the explosion. The achievement of Operation Chariot was acknowledged with the awarding of five Victoria Crosses to participants of the mission. 'Chariot' is still described as 'the greatest raid of all time'. British losses at St Nazaire were very high but the raid had crippled the Germans' ability to maintain their front-line warships.

Operation Ironclad

Also in 1942, the largest seaborne landings yet undertaken by the British were mounted against the Vichy French naval base at Diego-Suarez in Madagascar. Plans for taking the island were drawn up in March 1942 under the codename Operation Ironclad. Men of No. 5 Cdo were assigned as part of the assault force with the mission to come ashore a few hours ahead

The skills and tactics pioneered by army commandos in World War Two have continued with today's brigade when deployed in areas such as Iraq and Afghanistan. (MOD)

By 1941 commandos mounted raids at Vagsoy in Norway among some of the first operations after formation of the new force. (War Office)

of the main assault force and silence two artillery batteries. This task was successfully accomplished: the commandos took the Vichy French by complete surprise and captured some 300 prisoners. They then assisted in taking the port of Diego-Suarez.

Despite this early success, Churchill recognised that it was necessary to mount a larger-scale operation to gain further experience and expand the commando role before the main invasion of Europe could be launched. Initially, the men who formed the Cdo units had been drawn solely from Army regiments, but then on February 14, 1942 the first Royal Marine Commando, No. 40, was raised and more followed in 1943. The first Royal Marines units were titled with a number followed by the words 'Royal Marine Commando'. Then, in 1946 the titles changed to the unit number followed by 'Commando Royal Marines'.

In early 1942 with just one Royal Marine Commando unit in existence, the main body of the Royal Marines Corps provided manpower for ships of the Fleet, as well as operating a mobile Naval Base Defence Organisation. The latter force was deployed to Crete to build defences on the island following the British evacuation from Greece, but soon had to fight its way out after a major German air and seaborne invasion. Elsewhere a Royal Marines unit called 'Viper Force' was deployed to Rangoon for coastal patrolling. It also had to fight its way out after the Japanese invaded Burma in 1942.

A wounded commando officer is assisted by colleagues after a raid in Norway which included the Loften islands and Vagsoy island. (War Office)

A raid on December 27, Operation Archery, involved men from Nos. 2, 3, 4, and 6 Commandos. It caused significant damage to factories, warehouses, the German garrison, and also sank eight ships. (War office)

Lord Mountbatten, who was to be appointed head of Combined Operations and supported new raids in France at Dieppe and St Nazaire. (War Office)

The Combined Operations organisation was now beginning to take shape under Lord Mountbatten's direction, and amphibious equipment was slowly being improved. Within just six months of being raised, 40 RM Cdo saw its first action, but with almost disastrous results. The operation was officially described as a 'reconnaissance in force' and was planned to be no more than a 24-hour raid to see if a port deemed essential to the success of any invasion of Europe could be seized intact.

The fishing port of Dieppe was selected. This operation was considered essential because it would test the Allies' amphibious techniques. As planning continued, the main objective was still to assess the potential for seizing a port and evaluating Britain's amphibious capability. The raid, codenamed Operation Rutter was provisionally set for the night of June 20, 1942 but a rehearsal on the Dorset coast a week earlier, did not go well and a further period of training was considered necessary. A second rehearsal ➲

Back on board a Royal Navy warship after a raid in Norway, army commandos pose for a historic photograph. (War Office)

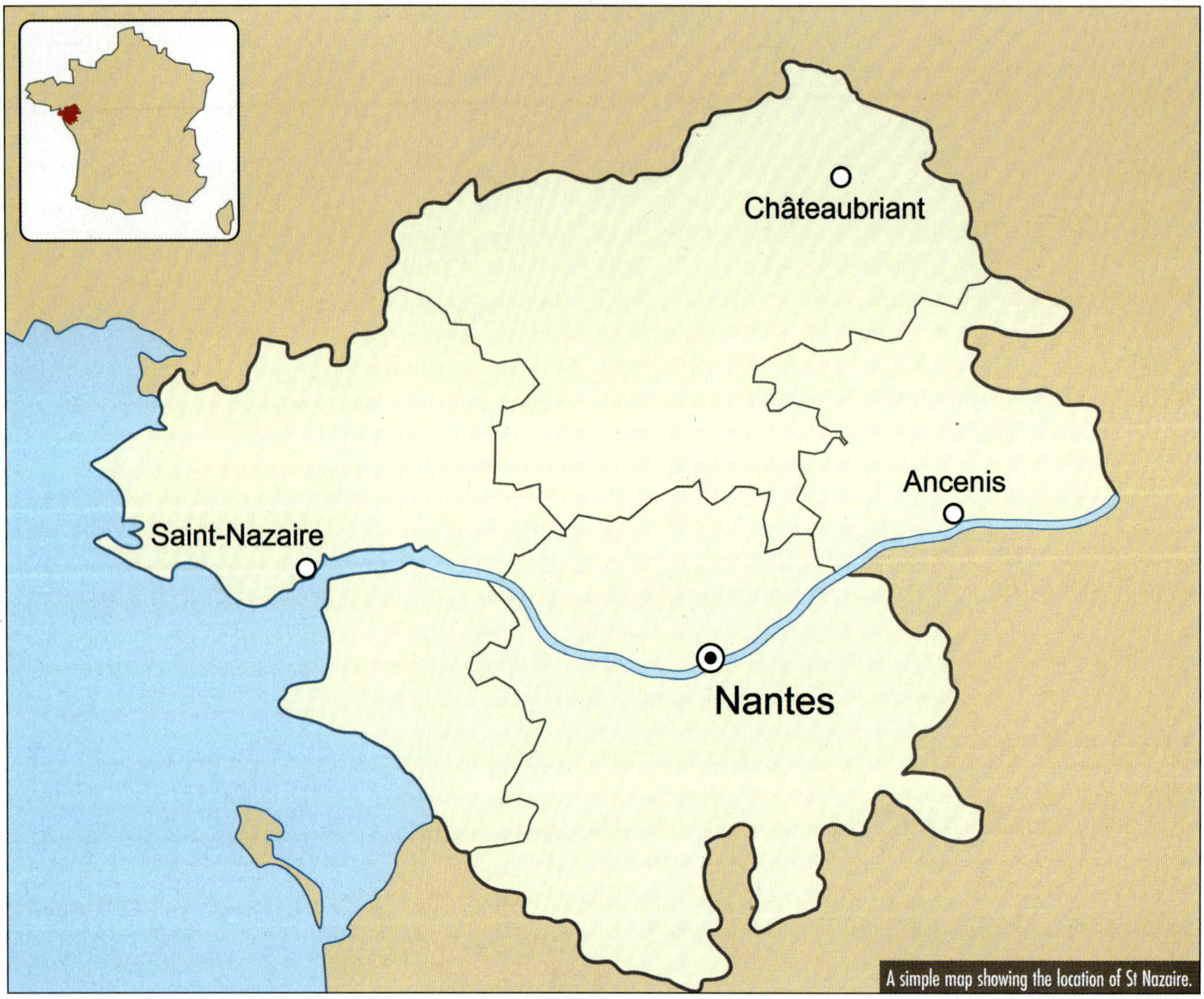

A simple map showing the location of St Nazaire.

at the end of June went much better. The raid was then rescheduled for early July, but the weather forced it to be cancelled - it was rescheduled for August and renamed Operation Jubilee.

Operation Jubilee

Since it was clear that the weather would be a critical factor, the idea of using parachute troops for the outer flanking landings was rejected, and Nos 3 and 4 Cdos were substituted. They would assault from the sea. It was also decided that because of the risk of heavy casualties among the French civilian population of Dieppe, there could be no preliminary bombardment from the air or by capital ships. The success of the plan would therefore rest entirely on surprise.

On the evening of August 18, the force weighed anchor and set sail from the shelter of the Solent. The forces employed at Dieppe were far larger than any used on previous raiding operations. The landing included six battalions of Canadian infantry and a Canadian tank regiment, three British commando units, including the newly formed Royal Marine Commando, elements of the US Rangers, men from No. 10 (Inter-Allied) Cdo, and a Royal Engineer unit.

This direct assault was charged with destroying German defences within the town, capturing German barges in the inner harbour, and sailing them back to England. The barges were to have been used in Hitler's Operation

Today's commandos come ashore in small boats during an exercise in Cornwall continuing the hallmark commando 'hit and run' tactics first used in the 1940s. (MOD)

Sealion plan to assault southern England. Further objectives included the destruction of radar installations, the airfield at St Aubin three miles inland of the port, and an attack on a German divisional HQ at Arques-la-Bataille, six miles inland. The time allotted for this ambitious operation from landing to withdrawal, was seven hours.

However, poor intelligence and a lack of reconnaissance failed to identify the strength of German fortifications in and around Dieppe, and while the Allies were aware of gun batteries that protected the sea approaches into the port, the level of reinforcement of these positions had been underestimated. The extent of their reinforcement was immense - they were in effect the first stage of Hitler's developing Atlantic Wall - and even today two of the bunkers on the left of the road are a reminder of the Dieppe operation.

HMS *Campbeltown* was stripped out and her bow packed with explosive charges which were fitted with timing devices designed to detonate hours after the ship rammed the gates of the St Nazaire dry-dock. (War Office)

Commandos in the 1940s had little specialist clothing or equipment. Soldiers wore heavy battle-dress uniforms, carried a Thompson sub machine gun, and a toggle rope. (War Office)

To secure the flanks, No. 3 Cdo's mission was to destroy the coastal defences and Goebbels battery in the area of Bernival, while No. 4 Cdo were to land on two beaches and destroy the Hess battery at Varengeville. The Royal Hamilton Regiment was scheduled to land at White Beach and 40 RM Cdo would go ashore in support of the Canadians. The beach in front of the town was made up of stone and shingle. It was also fairly steep. To this natural defence the Germans had added wire and mines. Additionally, it was shadowed by coastal guns which could trap any invaders in the water before they had time to get ashore.

H-hour for the first troops to land was 0450hrs on Wednesday August 19, 1942. All went well until 0345 hrs, when the invasion fleet was only seven miles from the French coast and still completely undetected. Then, quite without warning, a starshell illuminated the small group of landing craft carrying No.

3 Cdo onto Yellow Beach 1 at Berneval. They had run into a small German convoy and the element of surprise was totally lost. To make matters worse the battle had raised the alarm on shore. Only seven of the 23 craft carrying No. 3 Cdo managed to get ashore at Berneval, and of the men who landed, at least 120 were killed, wounded, or captured.

The six-gun battery near Varengeville was situated almost 1,000 yards inland from the beach and the guns above the cliffs were the target of No. 4 Cdo, commanded by Lieutenant Colonel the Lord Lovat. Earlier he had mounted rehearsals at Lulworth Cove in Dorset. Their task was to assault the guns with two forces. The planning and preparation paid off for Lovat and his men and their operation went well, although it was a very bloody assault. Lovat and his force made their way back to the rendezvous with their landing craft.

In Dieppe itself the advantage of surprise was lost. The cliffs on the flanks of the town were heavily defended and the main force, attempting to land on Dieppe beach with inadequate fire support, was badly mauled before it reached the shore. It was clear that all was not well, but details of what was actually happening were very difficult to obtain, not least because the beaches were obscured by the heavy smokescreen laid to shield the offshore fleet from the coastal batteries.

A decision was made to commit 40 RM Cdo to White Beach on the understanding that the Canadians had established a foothold and were doing well. Then it suddenly became clear that the Canadians had not secured White Beach and were in fact in serious trouble. It was decided that any attempt by HMS *Locust* and the Royal Marine Commandos to enter the port was to be abandoned, but the Marines on *Locust* were already attempting to close on Dieppe when the order was given. 40 RM Cdo prepared to land in support of the Canadian Royal Hamilton Light Infantry on White Beach, they quickly transferred from the French gunboats into assault landing craft and were escorted into Dieppe by HMS *Locust*.

The marines were now in seven landing craft with Lieutenant Colonel Joseph Picton-Phillips leading the way. The small force quickly ➲

HMS *Campbeltown* at the dry-dock where the warship rammed the dock. Hundreds of Germans climbed aboard and were killed when the explosives detonated. (War Office)

The commandos quickly adapted their uniform, wearing balaclavas on the cold raids in Norway and many wore Denison smocks. (War Office)

Wounded British commandos escorted by German guards – many commandos were executed on orders direct from Hitler. (German Archives)

came under accurate fire - a Royal Navy officer described the assault as a seaborne version of the Charge of the Light Brigade with shell blasts constantly hitting the waters around the flotilla as it made its way towards White Beach. Near the shoreline the firepower increased, and it became clear that any attempt to reach the beach would end in death, but the Colonel refused to turn back until he had made every possible effort to land. He knew the situation was hopeless. Enemy gunfire controlled every aspect of the beach and in an outstanding act of bravery Picton-Phillips put on a pair of white gloves and semaphored to the other assault boats to turn back. He was shot and killed in a matter of seconds.

Alan Saunders, who served with X Company, 40 RM Cdo, said: "As we approached the beach, I was firing my Bren, but we had little chance. The Canadians who had tried to make it in had been hit hard and the sea was full of burning landing craft and every few seconds another shell landed. It was hell.

"We wore battledress and steel helmets - the only action in which we wore them

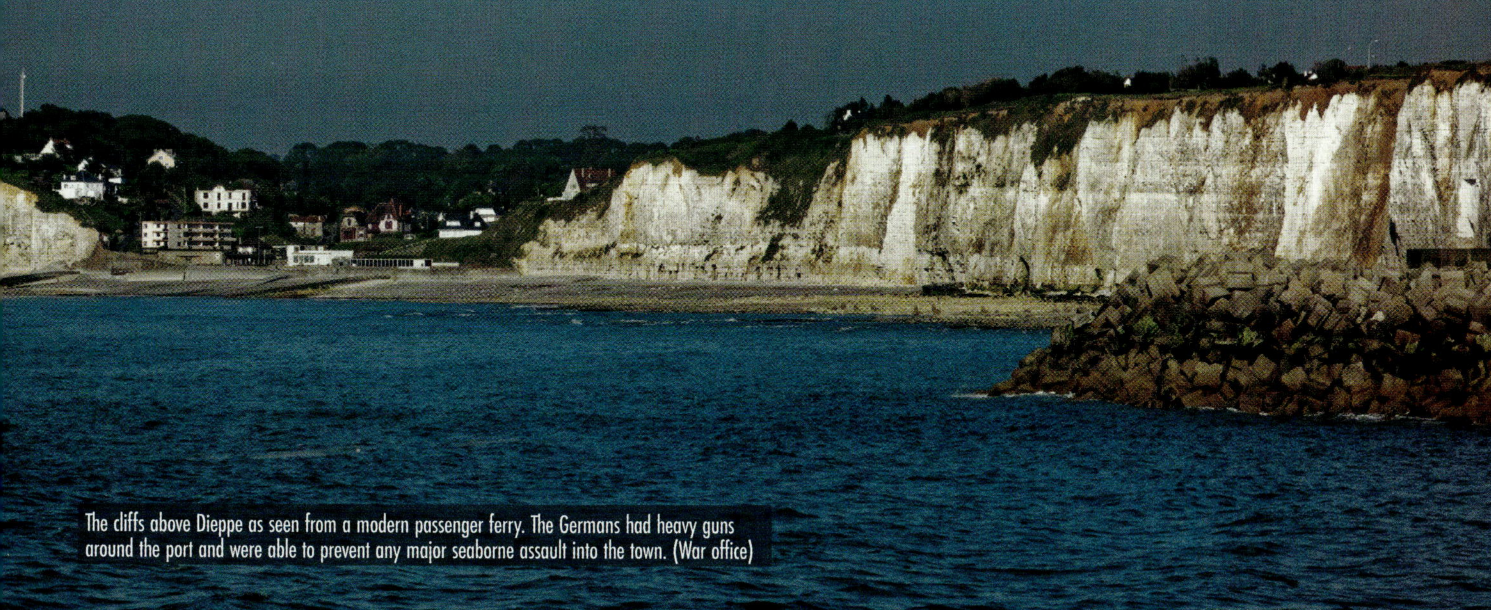

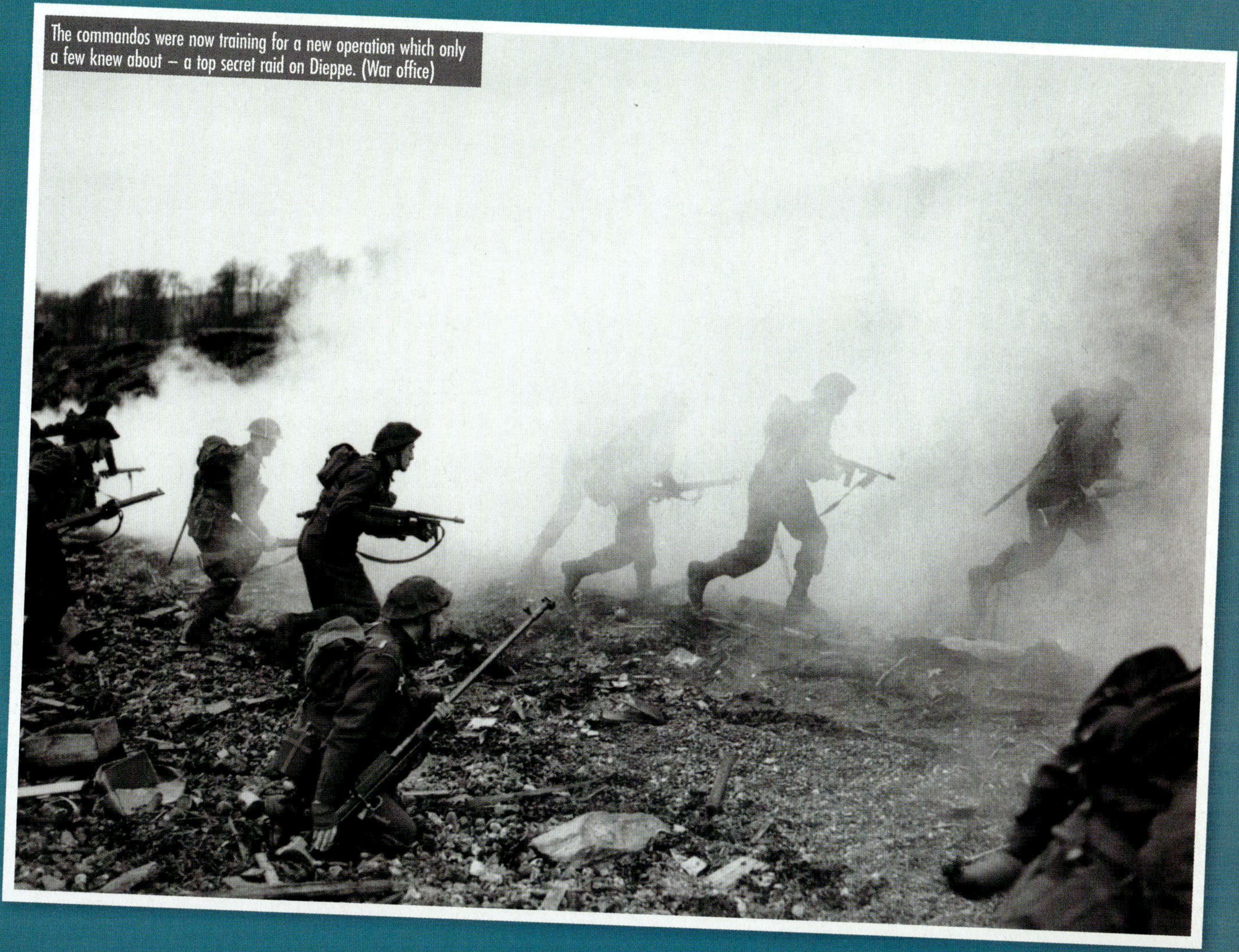

The commandos were now training for a new operation which only a few knew about – a top secret raid on Dieppe. (War office)

as I remember. We carried 100 rounds of ammunition, six grenades, a toggle rope and scaling ladders. We were just 200 yards off the shore when our LCA was hit and burst into flames. Some of us reached the shore, but realised there was nothing we could do but get the hell out of it. I can still see that scene in White Beach. It was bloody chaos, bodies floating everywhere, debris across the beach and the constant rattle of gunfire being aimed at us. I suppose you would call it the killing fields. I was in a group tasked to get into the German naval headquarters and secure sensitive papers which the intelligence boys had highlighted, but obviously it never happened. Our little group swam back out to sea and hung onto floating debris. We were picked up four hours later by HMS *Brocklesby* having ditched our ammo boots, helmets, and anything else that was too heavy. The ship picked up our Quarter Master Wiggie Bennett, who obviously looked after all our stores, and guess what? He was still wearing every bit of his kit including steel helmet and ammunition boots - we couldn't believe it."

60% Casualties

In human terms, with a casualty rate at Dieppe of more than 60% - the operation was a tragedy. However, the lessons learned were to prove vital to the success of the landings at Normandy two years later.

In 1943 Mountbatten was appointed Commander Southeast Asia and concentrated on the re-taking of Burma. The commandos played a vital role in the Arakan, the coastal region of Burma that offered a route to the centre of the country.

The cliffs above Dieppe as seen from a modern passenger ferry. The Germans had heavy guns around the port and were able to prevent any major seaborne assault into the town. (War office)

Hundreds of Canadian and British prisoners were taken by the Germans following the Dieppe raid, while hundreds were killed before they could get off the beaches and many more were wounded. (War Office)

The Dieppe raid and the constant stream of smaller commando operations infuriated Hitler and the German command. On October 18, 1942, the Führer had issued an instruction to his senior field officers which in essence directed that any commando soldier captured should be shot, whether he was carrying arms or not. The order was savagely implemented by the Germans who murdered many soldiers taken prisoner in the course of the war, including the Royal Marines captured on Operation 'Frankton' - the daring 'Cockleshell Heroes' canoe raid on shipping at Bordeaux. The canoe raid took place in December 1942. It was the first raid for the newly raised Royal Marines Boom Patrol Detachment: their mission was to canoe 71 miles up the Gironde River and attack German shipping. These enemy vessels were valuable and important targets as they were bringing in vital supplies from the Far East and the majority had evaded Royal Navy submarines.

By late 1942 there was a demand for more commandos, and under pressure from Lord Mountbatten, the Chiefs of Staff Committee broke up the Royal Marines Division and the Mobile Naval Base Defence Organisation and in April 1943 started to form them into commando units.

Achnacarry

The Commando Training Centre at Achnacarry near Fort William provided specialist training for army volunteers. The camp was isolated in the Scottish Highlands and provided the perfect location for a rugged and realistic training. The name Achnacarry quickly became known throughout the military. Following the establishment of the training centre, no soldier could join a commando unit or wear the coveted green beret without passing a six-week gruelling physical course. During the three years of its existence, thousands of troops from all regiments of the British Army, the Royal Marines, and Allied forces, completed the course. Captains Fairbairn and Sykes, two former Shanghai police officers, taught unarmed combat and designed the Fairbairn-Sykes fighting knife which was issued to all commandos. Achnacarry had a single aim - to produce fit, tough, disciplined soldiers who could work in small teams. Speed marching was a high priority, they covered, on average one mile every ten minutes, up to 12 miles, carrying full equipment and rifle. One of the tests volunteers faced was an endurance course that included a five-mile speed march followed by an assault course or a range test in which their shooting ability was measured. Today, the Commando Training Centre at Lympstone still uses this selection test, although in an adapted format. A memorial to all those who served with the wartime commandos sits at Spean Bridge.

A returning boat packed with commandos and a German prisoner. Dieppe had been a chaotic tragedy. It lacked intelligence and the support of heavy naval gunfire which had been stopped in case civilians were killed. (War Office)

Throughout this period, amphibious operations continued to be developed. In November 1942, the biggest amphibious operation to date took place: the invasion of Vichy French North Africa in Operation Torch. British and US seaborne landings took place along the coast from Casablanca to Algiers. While the landings, in which No. 1 Cdo took part, were lightly opposed, valuable experience was gained from their sheer scale. 'Torch' had been planned to link up quickly with the British 8th Army and capture Tunis, but in reality, progress was slow. The Germans flew in reinforcements from Sicily, and it was not until May 1943 that the Allies secured North Africa. There was now an urgent requirement to get a foothold in Europe.

The capture of Sicily, Operation Husky, was planned as a pincer movement, with the US 7th Army invading on the west coast between Licata and Scoglitti and the British 8th Army on the east coast south of Syracuse. Both 40 and 41 RM Cdo units were to land on the left flank of the Canadians, with No. 3 Cdo landing on the northeast extremity of the invasion, tasked to neutralise machine guns overlooking the beaches where the 5th Division was to land. The wealth of experience collected in the amphibious assaults in Norway, France, and Italy was to provide the knowledge necessary for the successful planning of the D-Day landings in June 1944. ●

Lord Lovat chats with some of his commandos on the return to Newhaven from Dieppe. (War Office)

Training at Achnarcarry was tough. The castle was remote, and the local surroundings provided the perfect location for the commando course. (War Office)

COMMANDOS AT WAR

The greatest amphibious assault in history, the Allied invasion of German-occupied Normandy, was launched on June 6,1944. It had taken four years to plan and commandos serving in the Special Service Brigades were at the forefront of the amphibious assault which punched a hole in the enemy's defences and that eventually provided the route to victory in Europe. Since Dunkirk in 1940, preparations had been under way for the invasion with Army and Royal Marine Commandos striking along the enemy-held coastline, mounting deception attacks to distract Hitler's commanders and, of course, launching the raid on Dieppe in August 1942, which provided valuable lessons for D-Day.

As planning for the 'main event' continued, in 1943 a number of raids were launched against the French coast, aimed at gathering intelligence and capturing prisoners who could provide vital information for the Allied assault. In autumn of the same year, further raids were made in Norway which forced the Germans to divert troops from their fortifications along the French coast, particularly in Normandy, to reinforce their units in parts of Norway. These attacks helped to confuse and distract the enemy and supported the overall deception plan intended to convince the German High Command that any Allied invasion would focus on the Calais area.

However, in spite of the deception plans, the preparation, and the experience of the previous four years, doubts still remained. An attack by US Marines in the previous November on the tiny Pacific island of Betio in the Tarawa Atoll reminded the Allies of the casualties that could be suffered in an assault on a well-defended beach. On an island the size of New York's Central Park the Marines lost more than 1,000 men and double that figure was wounded in a 76-hour running battle before the Japanese defenders were overcome. Tarawa and the legacy of Dieppe made it clear that it was essential that the first waves of commandos got ashore and off the Normandy beaches as quickly as possible.

The Commando Memorial is a listed monument dedicated to the original British Commando Forces raised during World War Two. It overlooks the training areas of the Commando Training Depot established in 1942 at Achnacarry Castle. (Fin Reynolds/DPL)

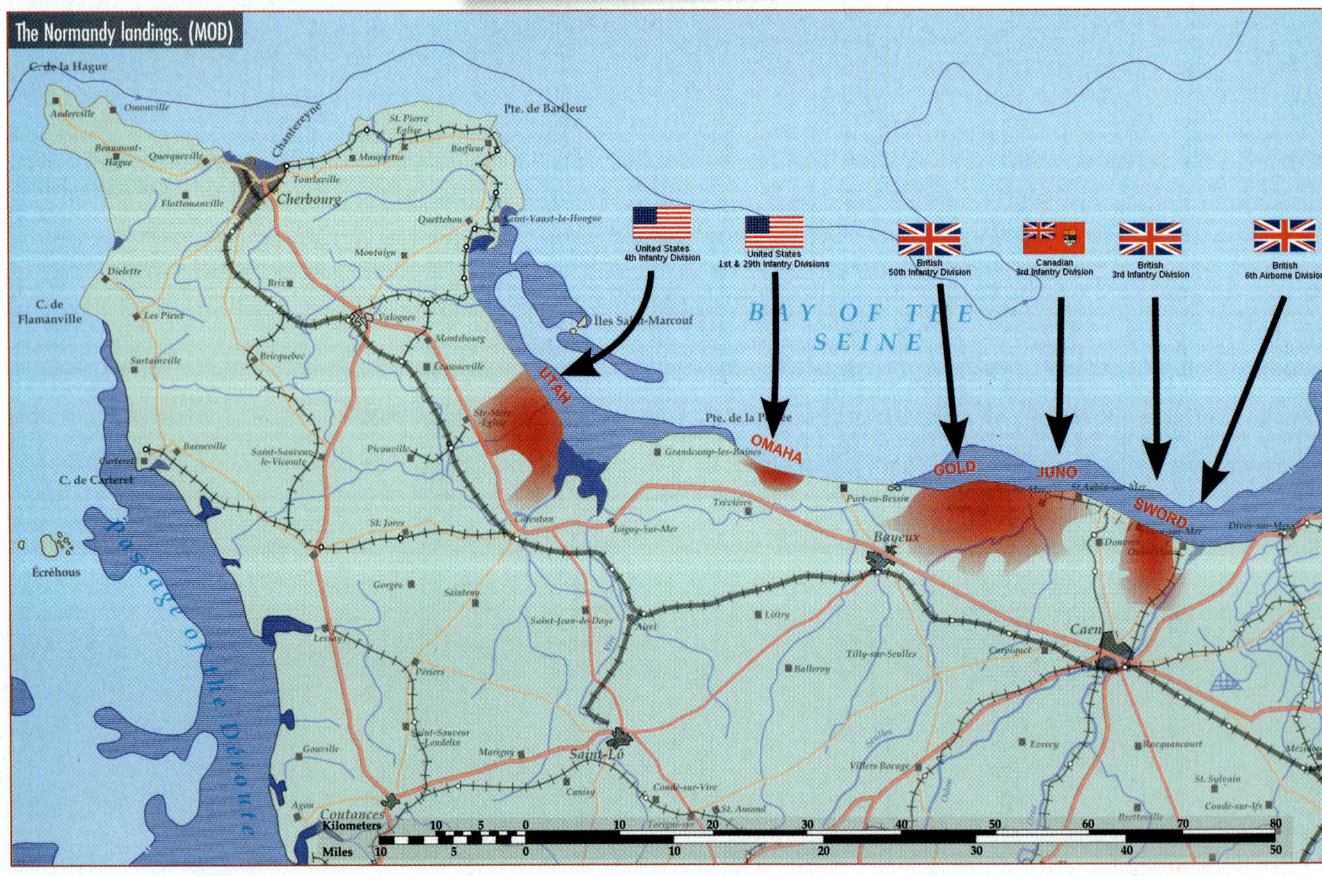

The Normandy landings. (MOD)

Today's commandos continue the spirit of their wartime forefathers who served across Europe. (MOD)

It was a dedicated Royal Marine brigade consisting of 41, 46, 47, and 48 RM Cdos. In total there would be three Army Commando and five Royal Marine Commando units taking part in the Normandy landings. At Normandy, the 1st and 4th Brigades were earmarked for quite different tasks.

The plan involved US and British airborne troops mounting a combined parachute and glider assault ahead of the commandos to secure and protect the flanks of the beach landings. They would also seize strategic objectives six miles inland and prevent the Germans from trapping the main assault force at the beachhead. Brigadier Lord Lovat was to land his 1st Brigade on Sword beach on the left flank and seize the port of Ouistreham before pushing forward through German lines to link up with the 6th Airborne Division inland. His force would subsequently come under the command of the airborne brigade. The men of 4th Special Service Brigade were deployed to the west of their colleagues in 1st Brigade and ordered to seize a number of coastal resorts at Lion-sur-Mer, St Aubin, Luc, and Langrune, as well as providing troops to extend and link the flanks of the British and Canadian landings on Gold and Juno beaches and towards the flank of the American landings on Omaha. 47 RM Cdo of 4th Special Service Brigade was to operate on the extreme right of the British Army, away from its brigade. Its mission was to seize the fishing town of Port-en-Bessin. 46 RM Cdo was to be the brigade reserve and would go ashore on June 7, the day after the main landings.

Marking the beaches

Before dawn on June 6, small units of naval commandos landed ahead of the main force to mark the landing sites and ensure that the assaulting units found their designated beaches, while off the coast of Normandy, Royal Navy midget submarines got into position on the surface ready to use their navigation lights to provide additional direction for the first assault waves. On D-Day, daybreak was at 0515hrs with sunrise listed in the orders as at 0600. It was a cold morning. The sea off Normandy was packed with landing craft and assault ships ➲

Army commandos aboard a landing craft on D-Day June 6, 1944 head for the beach. (War Office).

In May 1944, a troop from No. 10 Cdo carried out raids along the Pas de Calais coast to gain information on the types of mines being used by the Germans while at the same time continuing the deception plan that any invasion would strike at this part of France.

By 1944 the commandos were well organised and assigned to four Special Service Brigades (SS Bde). The 1st Special Service under the command of Brigadier the Lord Lovat was in Britain preparing for 'Overlord' and included Nos 3, 4, and 6 Army Cdos as well as 45 RM Cdo. The 2nd SS Bde was in the Mediterranean and consisted of Nos 2 and 9 Army Cdos as well as 40 and 43 RM Cdos. The 3rd SS Bde was about to depart for the Far East and included Nos 1 and 5 Army Cdos as well as 42 and 44 RM Cdos. Finally, 4th Special Service was also in the UK and preparing for D-Day under the command of Brigadier 'Jumbo' Leicester.

The Normandy landings had taken four years to plan and with commandos serving in the Special Service Brigades at the forefront of the naval assault. (War Office)

As planning for the operation continued, in 1943 a number of commando raids aimed at gathering intelligence were launched against the French coast. (War Office)

bobbing around as they headed towards their landing beaches. Gunfire support from battleships constantly pounded the enemy on shore. In the first 16 hours of the invasion 132,815 (75,215 British and Canadian and 57,600 American) troops were landed. Allied troops poured onto five beaches codenamed Sword, Juno, Gold, Omaha, and Utah.

At Gold beach, east of Omaha, 47 RM Cdo was to go ashore with the British 50th Division. Further east on Juno beach 48 RM Cdo would come ashore at St Aubin. Then between St Aubin and Ouistreham, 41 RM Cdo would land with the British 3rd Division, while 46 RM Cdo was held back as a reserve. The commanding officer of 47 Cdo, Lieutenant Colonel Charles Phillips,

There were concerns in the runup to D-Day. During landings on the Pacific island of Tawara the US Marines had lost more than 1,000 men and double that figure was wounded in a 76-hour running battle before the Japanese defenders were overcome. (US Marines)

Commandos were at the forefront of the naval assault — which punched a hole in the enemy's defences that eventually provided the route to victory in Europe. (War Office)

had the task of capturing the vital harbour of Port-en-Bessin where an undersea fuel pipeline would come ashore to supply the invasion force. His unit was the last of the commandos to land in France, but its mission was probably the most difficult. 47 RM Cdo was to land near Arromanches and march more than ten miles inland through enemy-held terrain to assault Port-en-Bessin from the rear. Corporal Ken Parker went ashore with 47 RM Cdo, he said D-Day was terrifying. He recalled: "As we sat there, I think it is fair to say that everyone was scared stiff. I'm not afraid to say that I almost wet my pants and I am sure a few prayers were said that morning. The firepower that the enemy put down was awesome and accurate. It was as if they were expecting us."

However, as the marine commandos broke cover they came under heavy sniper fire and while 47 Cdo was able to secure the port, the enemy troops mounted a fierce

Brigadier Lord Lovat's 1st Brigade landed on Sword beach on the left flank and seized the port of Ouistreham before pushing through German lines to link up with the 6th Airborne Division inland. (War Office)

The 1st Special Service Brigade linked up with airborne troops at Pegasus Bridge. (War Office)

48 RM Cdo suffered heavy losses with almost 40% of manpower being killed or injured. Lt Col Moulton's leadership gave his commandos the direction they needed. He walked up the beach, almost in defiance of the enemy shelling, he grouped his senior officers at the sea wall and began to take stock of the situation. Suddenly a mortar bomb landed close by, and splinters struck him in the arm, hand, and leg, but he chose to ignore the injuries and began sorting out his men, The unit set off for Langrune determined to meet up with 41 Cdo. The brigade commander, Brigadier Bernard 'Jumbo' Leicester, ordered the unit to stop and take up defensive positions in anticipation of an armoured counterattack. Landing on the Canadian Juno Beach, No. 48 Royal Marine Commando was the first commando unit to land near Saint-Aubin-sur-Mer and started the assault on Langrune-sur-Mer, which was liberated after heavy fighting and severe losses. They then held a position awaiting reinforcement and equipment to land. Major David Flunder, who was serving with 48 RM Cdo remembers the advance to Langrune and the sight of A Troop 48 RM Cdo led by its commander Major Mike Reynolds. In spite of being hit in both arms Reynolds led his troop ashore, his battledress soaked in blood. 'It was a quite remarkable sight', said Flunder.

The expected counterattack did not happen, and the next day Lt Col Moulton took what was left of his commando unit into Langrune to capture the strongpoint. When we took over our positions at Sallenelles from 4th Parachute Battalion they had just beaten off a heavy German attack and our first task was to clear up the battlefield and bury a substantial number of German corpses before settling down to improve our positions and start a programme of aggressive patrolling.

Many of the men in 41 RM Cdo had seen service in Italy and Sicily before returning to England to prepare for the Normandy landings. The unit had the task of assaulting Lion-sur-Mer on Sword beach - the most

counterattack, killing a number of marines and taking others prisoner. The following morning a recce patrol was sent in and discovered that the enemy had fled. The battle for Port-en-Bessin cost the lives of at least 60 Royal Marine Commandos and the local community has never forgotten its liberators. The survivors of 47 RM Cdo are regularly welcomed back and treated as dignitaries by the fishing community. As 48 RM Cdo went ashore at Juno it also met fierce opposition.

Lieutenant Colonel Jim Moulton had only taken command of 48 RM Cdo just 12 weeks before D-Day.

He ordered his mortars to fire smoke from the landing craft -using sandbags as a baseplate - and in a pitching sea hit the beach, sending clouds of smoke scudding down the shoreline to obscure the landing commandos from enemy fire. As the landing progressed,

Pegasus Bridge had been seized by glider troops. When the commandos marched over their piper Bill Millen played them across. (War Office)

Commandos of the 1st Special Service Brigade in Normandy. (War Office)

easterly of the three British beaches. On D-Day, 41 RM Cdo actually landed almost 200 yards west of the intended site. The plan involved the commando being split into two assault units. Force 1 was to neutralise the enemy strongpoint at Lion-sur-Mer, while Force 2 had the mission of assaulting a heavily defended château west of the town. The initial attack cost the lives of three officers, and it was a further 24 hours before the enemy position was captured by the Lincolnshire Regiment. The marines of 41 will always remember the death and destruction they saw as they landed. The regimental sergeant major was killed, and many commandos were fatally wounded. Nevertheless, the commando surrounded the radar station and with the assistance of a troop of tanks and forced 200 Germans to surrender.

On Sword beach was 45 RM Cdo and the green berets of the 1st Special Service Brigade commanded by Brigadier the Lord Lovat. Lord Lovat and his troops, who had been piped ashore by army commando Bill Millin. They quickly cleared the enemy out of Ouistreham and headed for the Bénouville bridge – later known as Pegasus Bridge. The airborne troops had secured the bridges and had fought off a German counterattack but were still under fire. Lovat's commandos reinforced the red berets and came under their command for the rest of the operation. 45 RM Cdo had been tasked to ➲

Securing the beaches was vital to allow stores and supplies to be ferried ashore to support the invasion force. (War Office)

The remains of the Mulberry harbour which still sits off the Normandy beaches.

Commandos left the beaches and headed towards Pegasus Bridge after landing on June 6, 1944. (War Office)

move inland to the village of Merville and occupy the nearby gun battery which had been captured after a fierce battle by the 9th Parachute Battalion. Two Royal Marines had in fact jumped with the battalion, Lieutenant Winston and Marine Donald who were to liaise between the two units.

On the morning of June 7 (D+1) 45 RM Cdo was ordered to take up positions around Hauger. Then later in the day the men were tasked to move again and seize the coastal defences at Franceville, which was situated on the far eastern side of the Orne estuary. This meant that they had to move back towards the coast past the Merville area. The target for 45 RM Cdo was the defences on the beach and those further east. The main road through Franceville was codenamed 'Piccadilly' and was to be a reference point for every commando in the unit during the assault. The advance to the village was bloody - the unit came under intense fire and sustained numerous casualties.

The commandos fought like lions, but faced a series of counterattacks from the Germans who were supported by heavy artillery. In the first

The commandos quickly seized German prisoners and passed them back to the Military Police to oversee. (War Office)

47 Commando had the task of capturing the vital harbour of Port-en-Bessin where an undersea fuel pipeline would come ashore to sustain the invasion force. (War Office)

The capture of beaches and ports allowed ships to come in close and deliver fuel, ammunition, and food. (War office)

three days of the Normandy campaign 45 RM Cdo suffered over 135 casualties including many killed.

46 RM Cdo went ashore on D+1 (7 June) as part of 4th Special Service Brigade. On June 11, the Commando liberated Rots and Le Hamel. As the invasion spread out from the French coast and supply lines lengthened, it became imperative to capture a major port if the 'breakout' were to maintain its momentum. The British and Canadians, for instance, were using 12,000 tons of supplies a day,

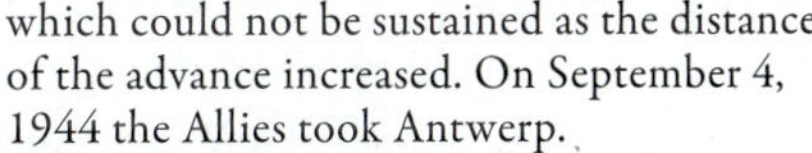
The commandos faced house to house fighting as they advanced through Normandy and beyond. (War office)

which could not be sustained as the distance of the advance increased. On September 4, 1944 the Allies took Antwerp.

Operation Infatuate

The liberation of Antwerp was a significant strategic success and allowed the Allies to maintain supply lines to the two million troops who were now advancing on Germany. However, there was a problem. The port sits on the River Scheldt, almost 40 miles inland from the sea. At the mouth of the river the huge estuary entrance to Antwerp was controlled by German fortifications

situated on the island of Walcheren. The force tasked to take Walcheren and the neighbouring islands consisted of 4th Special Service Brigade which was now made up of No. 4 Cdo, 41, 47, and 48 RM Cdos plus two troops of No. 10 Cdo. The assault, Operation Infatuate, was scheduled for November 1, with No. 4 Cdo landing to take the town of Flushing. The Royal Marine Commandos of 41, 47, and 48 landed at the western side of the island, tasked to assault, seize Westkapelle and destroy the coastal batteries. The commandos' raid on Walcheren was truly of David and Goliath proportions - the

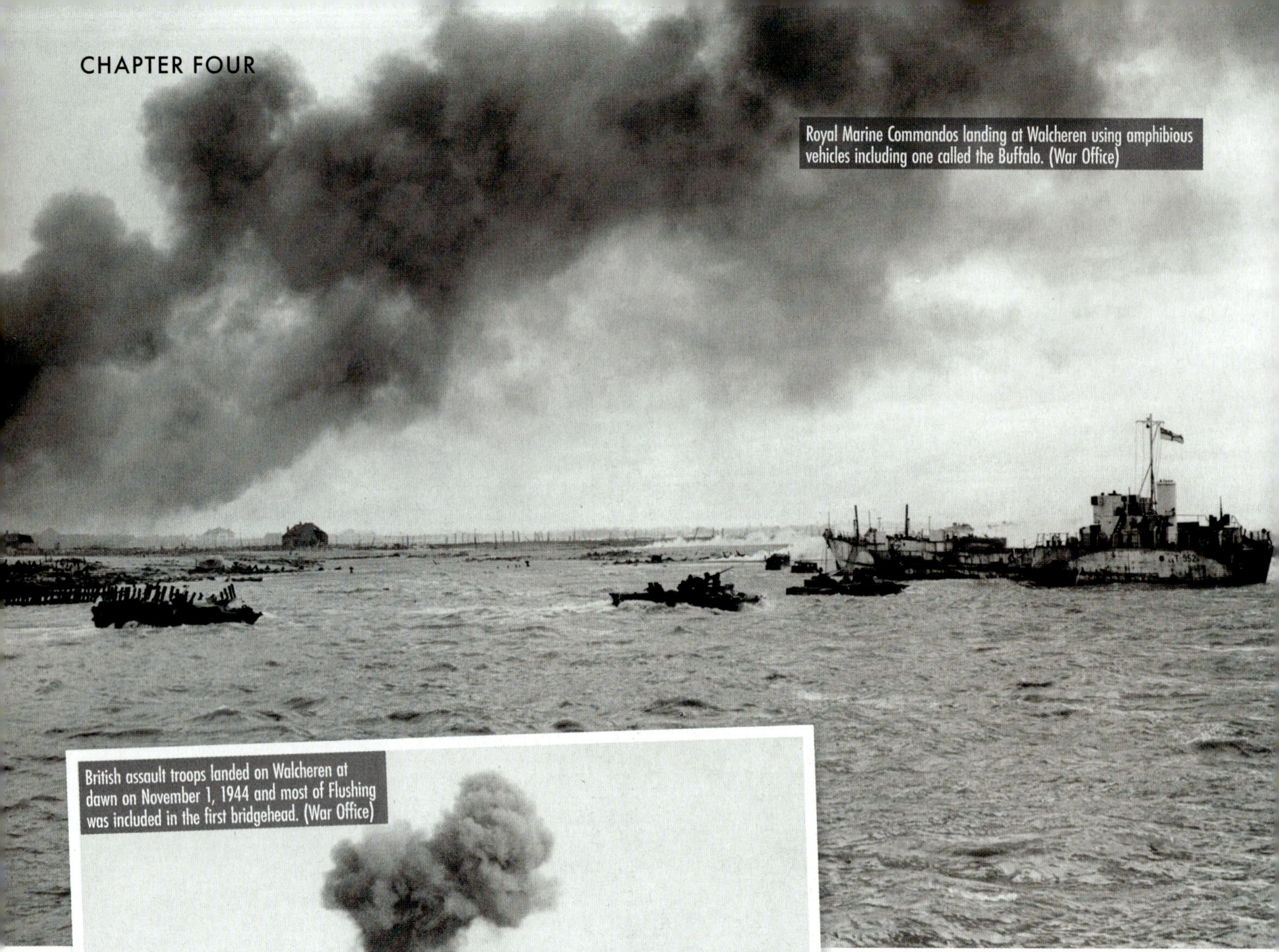
Royal Marine Commandos landing at Walcheren using amphibious vehicles including one called the Buffalo. (War Office)

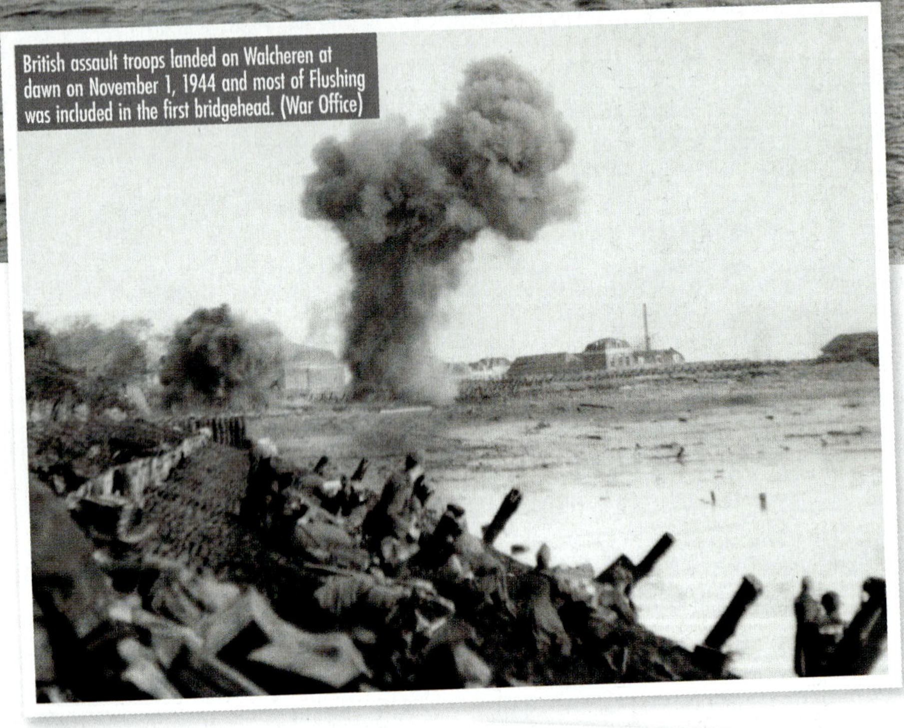
British assault troops landed on Walcheren at dawn on November 1, 1944 and most of Flushing was included in the first bridgehead. (War Office)

The commandos continued their advance and in March 1945 the first units crossed the Rhine. In early April, No. 1 Cdo Brigade reached Munster and two weeks later the brigade arrived in Luneberg and prepared for their final assault - a night crossing of the River Elbe, which runs across Germany from Hamburg to Dresden.

Italy and the Far East

During the winter of 1944, the Allied campaign in Italy had ground to a halt along a front just south of Bologna. The Allied plan called for a push northwest to Ferrara by the British 8th Army, using the Argenta Gap, which lay

Germans with their long-range gun batteries built into strong defences looking out to sea and the Allied force in a variety of landing craft and small ships.

The enemy blasted the assault force as it approached the shore and 172 Marines and sailors were killed, with a further 200 injured. The result was one of the bloodiest fights the commandos had ever faced, with 41, 47, and 48 RM Cdos landing under heavy fire. Landing in the Westkapelle area, 41 captured the town before advancing north to attack the coastal battery strongpoints. Nos 48 and 47 advanced south to link up with No.4 in the Zouteland area. After Westkapelle, No. 41 fought their way along the coastal strip to Domburg, where the other three commandos joined them, before pushing on to Vroumonpolder where the Germans capitulated and surrendered on November 8.

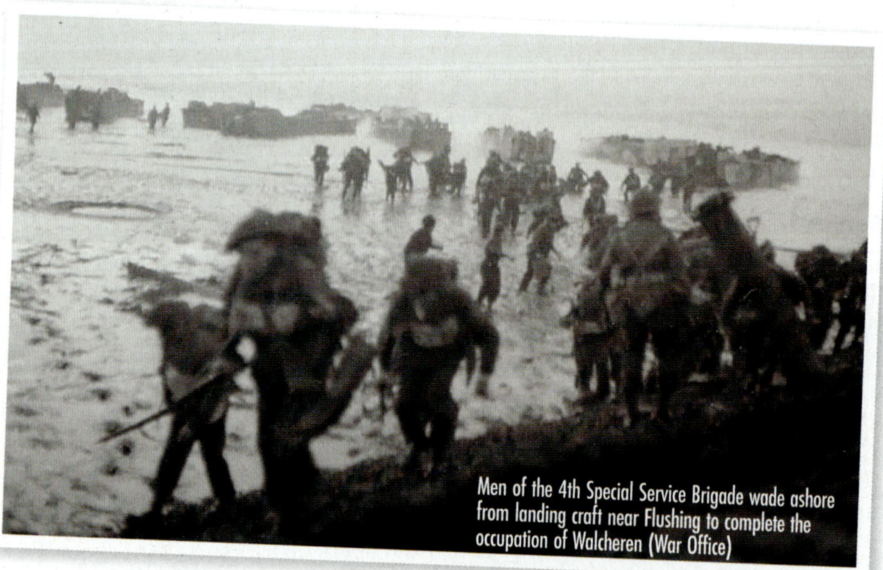

Men of the 4th Special Service Brigade wade ashore from landing craft near Flushing to complete the occupation of Walcheren (War Office)

Commandos of the 4th Special Service Brigade went ashore from landing craft near Flushing to complete the occupation of Walcheren in 1944. (War Office)

craft transported 42 RM Cdo to the landing beaches, which were secured with little opposition, and then No. 5 Army Cdo moved inland to root out the enemy. The brigade's other two units, No. 1 Army Cdo and 44 RM Cdo, were put ashore on the wrong beach but eventually got into action. The brigade was to surround the village of Kangaw. Where it faced fierce fighting. Nothing in the campaigns across Europe or North Africa could have prepared the commandos for the fanaticism of the Japanese, who mounted wave after wave of reckless attacks. They had almost no regard for human life and their soldiers were prepared to do anything for their country. The war had blooded the commandos who would now see the role assigned to the Royal Marines who would face more operations in the Far East. ●

between extensive floodlands to the west and the lagoons of Lake Comacchio on the eastern coast. The US 5th Army was to strike north to the west of Bologna. In order to weaken resistance in Bologna, a small British commando force was to strike first at Lake Comacchio, drawing reserves away to the east to ensure that before the 8th Army began its advance the threat posed to its right flank by enemy forces positioned around the lake was removed.

And in Burma, both 42 and 44 RM Cdos took part in the bitter fighting at Akyab, Myebon and Kangaw, as well as raids along the Arakan coast. Early in January 1945, No. 3 Cdo Brigade was ordered to carry out an amphibious assault against the Japanese forces holding the Myebon peninsula in northwest Burma. On January 12, assault

A Royal Navy landing craft with Royal Marine Commandos embarked heads to Walcheren at Westkapple, the most western point of the island. (War Office)

Modern day commandos have constantly evolved their tactics, but they base their ethos on the success of the wartime units who served at Walcheren, Lake Comacchio and in the Far East. (MOD)

THE POST-WAR YEARS

The equipment and weapons used by today's commandos is significantly advanced compared to the weapons used by 41 Independent Commando in Korea. (MOD)

A t the end of World War Two, the army force was disbanded, as were many Royal Marines units, and the 'commando role' assigned to the Royal Marines Commandos, who operated one brigade which included supporting British Army units of Royal Engineers and the Royal Artillery. Within a couple of years, conflict in the Far East would see the Royal Marines Commandos back in action in Korea, then Suez, Cyprus, Malaya, and Aden.

The post-war agreement to partition Korea and split control between the superpowers created political and social instability that ultimately led to conflict in 1950. The invasion by the Soviet-backed North Korean People's Army (NKPA) across the 38th Parallel signalled the start of a bitter three-year conflict that resulted in the deployment of

Royal Marine Commandos fighting alongside their colleagues in the US Marines in the most extreme weather conditions. A World War Two agreement had been formalised in which America would administer Korea until such time as the country could recover from Japanese rule and form its own government. A hasty and perhaps crude decision was made to divide Korea at the 38th Parallel, cutting the peninsula in two. The Soviets would control the north and the US would hold the south. In June 1949 North Korean forces rolled across the border and invaded the south. The United Nations called on its member states to render military assistance to the south and the United States immediately agreed. In London, Prime Minister Clement Attlee offered military force which would include the Royal Marines Commandos.

US forces quickly arrived as did the British 27th Infantry Brigade. The first British Royal Marines to serve in Korea (drawn from ships' detachments) also arrived at this time. They came from the Far East Fleet and the small team included six sailors. After initial training they were attached to a US Army raiding company. This first force was commanded by Lieutenant Derek Pounds who flew out from the UK to head the detachment, which later became known as 'Pound force'. The men spent three weeks training at Camp McGill, a US Army base at Takehama near the US naval base of Yokosuka, 50 miles south of Tokyo. Here the team was issued with US clothing and taught how to handle American weapons.

41 Commando reborn

At the time, 3 Commando Brigade was already heavily engaged in the anti-terrorist campaign in Malaya. The conflict had sprung up in June 1948, after Britain declared a state of emergency in Malaya which followed attacks on plantations which had themselves been revenge attacks for the killing of left-wing activists. The leader of the Malayan Communist

US Marines and Royal Marines Commandos deployed to Korea cook their rations in the freezing weather. (US Marines)

Party and his allies fled into the jungles and waged a war against British colonial rule. It was a savage conflict in which the commandos quickly became adept at living in the jungle. But Malaya had committed the Corps and a small independent commando unit for operations in Korea: 41 Commando was reborn, having been disbanded at the end of the World War Two.

In Plymouth, the base of the Royal Marines, orders were received in August 1950 to form an independent commando unit to serve with the United Nations forces deployed in Korea. The unit was to operate with US forces and undertake special raiding tasks behind enemy lines. It would be commanded by Lieutenant Colonel Douglas Drysdale and later be known as Task Force Drysdale. An initial force of 100 was raised from Royal Marines at establishments across the UK - an additional 100 had already sailed for the Far East. Drysdale and his unit started their journey to Japan on September 1, 1950, bound for Camp McGill. Those who flew out to Japan had to travel in civilian clothing and went via Cairo, Basra, Karachi, Rangoon, and Hong Kong. All were under strict orders not to appear as a military party so as not to cause a 'political incident'. Once in Hong Kong, the party changed into military uniform because the last legs of the journey were over allied-held territory. Those from the troopship soon joined them. The force was to be under

US and Royal Marines near Hagaru-ri. The weather conditions of the Korean winter were extreme and added to the challenge. (US Marines)

US Navy warplanes drop napalm on Korean forces. (US Navy)

command of the US Navy and at Camp McGill the commandos were issued with US clothing.

By the end of September, 41 Independent Commando embarked in a US submarine and two assault destroyers heading for the coast of North Korea. At this time, the North Koreans made a second attempt to seize Pusan and were significantly south of the 38th Parallel and in strong numbers. After conducting various raiding operations up and down the Korean coast, 41 Commando were shipped via sea transport to the port of Hungnam in North Korea to serve with the US First Marine Division as an additional reconnaissance unit. Their mission was to locate and destroy enemy forces on the left flank ranging as far as 23 miles west of Koto-ri. It was hoped that the British unit and the Divisional Reconnaissance Company might flush out the communist troops beyond the reach of infantry patrols. 41 Independent Commando were based a few miles inland at Hamhung where they remained for several days for fresh supplies, equipment, and cold weather clothing.

As winter set in the situation was getting more critical by the day. Communist Chinese forces had now entered the fighting and were furiously pressing home an attack at Hagaru-ri and Yudamni. There was only one US Marine infantry battalion at Hagaru-ri and when 41 Independent Commando arrived at Koto-ri, they were greeted with the news that the road to the north was blocked. Task Force Drysdale was directed to clear the road and to reinforce Hagaru-ri.

On November 29, on a cold, snowy morning, with the temperature hovering near zero, the Task Force set off from Koto-ri to Hagaru-ri on one of the most astonishing rescue operations in military history. It included 41 Commando, a US Marine company, and Baker company a ➲

A restored F4 Corsair in the Korean-era markings of the US Marine Corps. The Corsair was used in the fighter-bomber role throughout the conflict. (US Marines)

Marines in Korea near Chosin reservoir where the First Marine Division was trapped by Chinese forces. (US Marines)

British and American marines near Chosin reservoir wearing specially issued coats to combat the extreme cold. (US Marines)

communist Chinese opened fire from the right flank. There were Chinese in front of them, to the flanks and the rear, but they pushed on slowly around roadblocks and other obstacles. Halfway to Hagaruri, they reached Hell Fire Valley, a long valley in a mountainous range with a frozen creek winding through it. They were being bombarded everywhere and made next to no progress. Eight tanks arrived to support them, and it was decided that they should depend on the tanks and close air support to keep the flanks clear while the task force pushed through on trucks as quickly as possible.

The column pressed on with George Company, then 41 Commando, then Baker Company, and finally the transport vehicles. Heavy mortar fire continued, and once again the column had to stop. Casualties were now mounting and Lt Col Drysdale himself was wounded.

Communications were lost and the situation was desperate. American Corsair fighters attacked the Chinese during daylight to relieve the pressure, but they could not operate at night.

George Company, the US Marine force, could now see the lights at the Hagaru-ri airstrip where American engineers were working feverishly. After ten hours and an average of one mile an hour, they reached the Hagaru-ri perimeter – still under intense Chinese attacks. 41 Commando, the next in line to try to reach Hagaru-ri, took a blast when a mortar shell hit an ammunition truck at the end of the column. The blast formed a road-block, and 41 Commando was now cut off from Baker Company following behind. The Chinese launched an attack on 41, but despite heavy casualties, the Royal Marines held them off and pushed their way through three more roadblocks. At around 1.30 in the morning, they dragged themselves into Hagaru-ri. It was a bloody battle, but in the end, the commandos of '41' had made it to Hagaru-ri.

Breakout

General MacArthur, commander in chief of the UN forces, now facing a totally different situation, radioed Washington: In his opinion the force at his disposal was not sufficient to meet what was an undeclared war by the Chinese. He reported that the command had

US Army infantry unit. Air support was delayed because of poor visibility, and it was mid morning when they departed. The plan was that 41 Commando would take the first hill to the east of the road; the US Marines would take the second hill and Baker Company, would remain on the road to parallel the progress of the two units as they secured the high ground.

The size of the communist force ahead was quickly apparent, they were attacking in all different directions and destroying everything and everyone in their path.

Three communist Chinese divisions attacked the 5th and 7th Marines at Yudam-ni. Other elements attacked US forces holding Toktong Pass and the main supply route was cut in several places. At Hagaru-ri, near Chosin Reservoir, the US Marines and soldiers were completely surrounded and there was no place to turn. The task force now made up a convoy of almost 100 vehicles and several tanks. They moved north with little opposition until suddenly the

Royal Marines from 41 Independent Commando wearing US Marine clothing and armed with American weapons. (US Marines)

The British Commandos took their green berets with them and underwent training on US weapons. (US Marines)

US Marines Corsairs deliver close air support in a low-level attack on Chinese forces operating in Korea. (US Marines)

The Royal Marine Commandos were praised by the US Marines for their work in Korea and even today the two organisations maintain a close bond. (MOD)

done everything humanly possible within its capabilities but now was faced with conditions beyond its control and its strength. MacArthur was going over to the defensive, and Washington had no choice but to concur. There was only one option for Major General Oliver Smith and his marines and that was to fight their way out.

The breakout south from Hagaru-ri began early on the morning of December 6. The 7th Marines was ordered to take the lead, followed by the 5th Marines, with 41 Commando and the 3rd Battalion, 1st Marines attached. It was freezing and the wind made conditions worse. Damaged trucks, jeeps, and tanks littered the road. It took 38 hours to walk 11 miles, there were some vehicles but not enough. The 2nd Battalion, 7th Marines was the first to arrive at Koto-ri. The Chinese were still attacking the main column from both flanks, and they were pouring in everything they had. The marines retaliated in kind. Late on December 11, all units arrived in Hungnam. The US tanks which had escorted the force rolled in later. The US Marines thanked the Royal Marines for their valiant efforts – the Chosin Reservoir fight was over.

The Eastern Mediterranean

The Suez operation in 1956 was an Anglo-French mission, well planned and well executed by means of an airborne and amphibious operation as well as significantly the first helicopter assault by the commandos. But the mission's duration was short - British and French politicians buckled under the weight of international criticism and pulled their troops out.

After World War Two, British troops remained in Egypt, although forces prepared to withdraw as part of an agreement to remove troops from Cairo, Alexandria, and the Nile Delta by March 1947.

In July 1956, Egyptian President Gamal Abdel Nasser nationalised the Suez Canal Company, which at the time was a

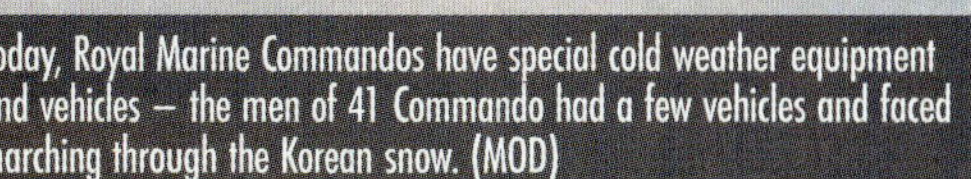
Today, Royal Marine Commandos have special cold weather equipment and vehicles – the men of 41 Commando had a few vehicles and faced marching through the Korean snow. (MOD)

The Royal Marines mounted the first helicopter assault at Suez flying from a Royal Navy carrier. It was a total success, although after a few days the force was ordered to withdraw. (MOD)

to within ten miles of the Suez Canal. Under the pretext of protecting the canal, Britain and France landed troops a few days later on November 5, 1956.

A political decision was made to land military force at Port Said, but amphibious shipping was in short supply, and it was more than 12 months since the units of 3 Commando Brigade had been able to mount an amphibious exercise. – due to a shortage of amphibious vessels. The concept of mounting helicopter assaults from carriers offshore had been put forward and now it was to be used in an operational role for the first time. On October 31, 1956, British and French air forces began attacks on Egyptian bases and virtually destroyed the country's air wing in 48 hours. The invasion plan was based on an amphibious assault, supported by relatively small numbers of British and French parachute troops. The paras faced the same problem as the marines - a lack of equipment, in their case aircraft. The seaborne landings were timed to begin on November 6 and were to coincide with the airborne drop, but at

joint British-French enterprise which had owned and operated the waterway since its construction in 1869. Nasser's announcement came following months of mounting political tensions between Egypt, Britain, and France. Nasser offered full economic compensation for the company, but the British and French were suspicious of his intentions and outraged at Egypt's state control of the canal. The Egyptian leader, in turn, resented what he saw as European efforts to perpetuate their colonial domination. The British and French held secret military consultations with Israel, who regarded Nasser as a threat to its security, resulting in the creation of a joint plan to invade Egypt and overthrow its President. In keeping with these plans, Israeli forces attacked across Egypt's Sinai Peninsula on October 29, 1956, advancing

At the height of the Suez crisis, commandos flew into Port Said aboard helicopters, in what was an ambitious first for the navy's Fleet Air Arm helicopter pilots. (MOD)

Royal Navy helicopters fly into Port Said during the Suez Crisis. The operation provided the evidence for the Royal Navy to develop the concept of helicopter assault. (MOD)

the last moment the parachute assault was brought forward by 24 hours. The airborne assault force was to fly in from Cyprus, while 45 Commando RM was to fly in aboard helicopters with 42 and 40 Commando and 2nd Battalion the Parachute Regiment, as well as supporting armour, landing by sea. The operation was a success, but political opposition led by the US forced the British and French to withdraw from the area within days. The Royal Marines lost ten men and a further 50 were wounded.

Trouble had flared in Cyprus in the mid-1950s and as 42 Commando RM returned

Helicopters on the deck of HMS *Theseus* during the Suez Crisis, smoke can be seen rising from Port Said following air strikes. (MOD)

Since the first use of helicopters for airborne assault at Suez, the use of rotary aviation has become common with the commandos using the platform to abseil from. (Patrick Allen /DPL)

home to the UK after Suez, both 40 and 45 Commandos were redirected to the island ready to mount internal security duties as the continued unrest escalated. Within months they would be fighting terrorists who were campaigning for British withdrawal from the island. Also, within a couple of years, the small British protectorate of Aden on the southern tip of the Red Sea saw conflict in 1963 when Arab nationalists sought the removal of the colonial administration.

Situated more than 60 miles north of Aden, the Quteibi, Ibdali and Bakri tribes traditionally supplemented their income by looting travellers on the Dhala road which connected Aden to the state of Yemen. In the mid-'60s, with the support of extremists from an organisation called the National Liberation Front (NLF), they were armed and willing to join the struggle to force the British to withdraw from the colony.

On St George's Day, April 23, 1960, 45 Commando RM arrived in Aden having

Aden had been under colonial administration for many years but in 1963 Arab nationalists wanted independence. (Jack Wiliams/DPL)

Men of B Troop 45 Commando pictured in Aden during their deployment in the 1960s. (MOD)

seen action at Suez in 1956 followed by two operational tours in Cyprus. The commandos went to Little Aden to relieve an army battalion and was tasked to guard the BP oil refinery next to the camp. Just a year after deploying to Aden, the unit was sent to Kuwait in response to a threatened invasion by Iraq. After three weeks 45 Commando, working alongside 42 Commando and other units, had restored order. It then returned to Aden.

Next, in January 1964, the unit embarked in the aircraft carrier HMS *Centaur* and sailed 1,500 miles south to Tanganyika in Africa where the army had revolted. The commandos quickly gained control, and as the politicians negotiated the unit again returned to Aden to resume guarding the oil refinery at Little Aden. But opposition to the British

Today, Royal Marines Commandos are deployed in the Middle East in anti-drug smuggling operations and sometimes to the Gulf of Aden where their forefathers were based. (MOD).

Many British military operations in Aden were mounted from a base the army built in an area called Radfan. (MOD)

The commandos used RAF Bristol Belvedere helicopters when operating in Aden's mountainous Radfan area. (DPL)

presence in the protectorate was growing and finally exploded into violence in 1963 when a bomb attack was made on the British High Commissioner. Violence became a daily occurrence, eventually families of military personnel were sent home and politicians agreed to withdraw the British presence. The withdrawal from Aden was originally planned for 1968 but was brought forward to November 29, 1967. In order to keep the airport out of the range of terrorist small arms fire, 45 Commando and 1st Battalion the Parachute Regiment held a line north of Sheikh Othman to cover the withdrawal. One by one, the units flew out. 45 Commando left at midnight on November 28, aboard a fleet of 13 RAF Hercules C-130s.

The following day 42 Commando left by helicopter and landed on HMS *Albion* which was offshore; it was the last unit to leave Aden. Twelve Royal Marines are buried at Ma'alla cemetery, and the grave of Marine Dunn lies at the British military cemetery in Silent Valley, Little Aden, just a mile or so from 45 Commando's former camp. In 1998 Major General Andrew Keeling returned to the country for a remembrance service and placed poppies on the graves. ●

THE FALKLAN

On April 2, 1982 Argentinian troops invaded the Falklands, a small British dependency in the South Atlantic. (DPL)

O n April 2, 1982 Argentinian troops invaded the Falklands, a small British dependency in the South Atlantic. A long-running claim by the South American country to sovereignty over the islands had finally erupted after General Leopoldo Galtieri was appointed President and announced that his administration would undertake to recover 'the Malvinas', by military force if necessary. At the time, Argentina's economy was in meltdown and Galtieri saw this as an opportunity to raise the country's morale and, more importantly, encourage support for himself.

Royal Marines Commandos who had served in previous detachments of Naval Party 8901, the Falkland Islands Royal Marine unit, were well aware of Argentina's claim and over the years there had been several 'significant incidents' that had inflamed the political situation, as well as 'intelligence indicators' that an invasion or landing force might take place. These continued, including on one occasion sending HMS *Chichester* to the South Atlantic after an Argentine warship fired across the bow of a British scientific research vessel that the Argentines believed was carrying Lord Shackleton.

In 1975, the British government had announced that the ice patrol ship HMS *Endurance* was to be withdrawn from the region and, while the decision was later revoked, it had clearly sent a message to Argentina that Britain was reducing her military commitment and her responsibility in the area. Then in 1977, British intelligence indicated that it believed that the Argentines could be planning to mount a landing on Southern Thule and the government tasked the Ministry of Defence to respond. The Royal Navy deployed the 'Leander'-class

DS CONFLICT

Within days of the Argentinian invasion, the Prime Minister Margaret Thatcher ordered a task force headed by HMS *Invincible* and HMS *Hermes* to the South Atlantic. (DPL)

The task force carriers sent to retake the Falkland Islands were packed with marines and stores offering little room on the journey south. (DPL)

frigate HMS *Phoebe*, the Type 21 frigate HMS *Alacrity*, the support ships RFA *Resource* and REA *Owen*, as well as the nuclear submarine HMS *Dreadnought*. Codenamed Operation Journeyman the mission was planned to provide a significant British naval presence in the South Atlantic. The operation was classified as top secret; the crew were sworn to secrecy and the incident was only revealed to the Commons in March 1982 at the height of the tension between the UK and Argentina. By mid-1981 the very mention of the word 'Falklands' was enough to prompt tired yawns from most British politicians. This reaction ➲

A Harrier jet lifts off from the Royal Navy aircraft carrier HMS *Invincible* on the way to the Falklands. (DPL)

Brigadier Julian Thompson (right), commander of 3 Commando Brigade with his planning team. (DPL)

was perhaps not surprising as the dispute over the islands had dragged on for decades with no conclusion in sight. But Britain seems to have assessed wrongly in 1981 that the subject of sovereignty had slipped off the political agenda in Argentina – it had not.

On March 24, an Argentine survey ship called the *Bahia Paraiso* entered Leith harbour on the island of South Georgia to land around 50 Argentines posing as scrap metal workers. However, under the cover of the supposed

At Ascension Island the commandos took the opportunity to undertake some last-minute training. (DPL)

civilian operation, the Argentine government actually landed a full-size naval infantry detachment led by Captain Alfredo Astiz. With HMS *Endurance* in the area, tensions mounted and the chances of an international incident soared. The Argentines reviewed their invasion plans and, in late March Galtieri directed two Argentine warships to reinforce the *Bahia Paraiso*.

In response to the Argentinian actions on South Georgia, the Royal Navy despatched three nuclear submarines to the region as Argentina prepared for an immediate invasion of the Falkland Islands. The Argentines had planned to mount an amphibious landing on April 1, but bad weather delayed their plans by 24 hours.

First Contact

Shortly after 0600hrs on April 2, the Argentine special forces unit, the Buzo Tactico, swept through the Royal Marine barracks in the Falklands' capital of Port Stanley and made for Government House. As they advanced, additional Argentine units moving through Stanley came under intense attack from various groups of commandos who had pre-positioned themselves to ambush the invaders. George Gill, a Royal Marine sniper takes up the story: "We heard the first explosions at around 0555hrs and they were

The car ferry MV *Norland* which had been requisitioned for the task force was subject to some very close misses. (DPL)

on our position about five or ten minutes later. They came very close, possibly about 30 metres before the firefight with us started. Suddenly six of them [Buzo Tactico] came over the back wall at Government House where three of the lads were waiting and they dropped three of them straight away. Three

others ran away in the darkness. They were about 10 feet away from each other and it was a case of just pull the trigger. We had no intention of giving up. Quite the opposite - we wanted to fight to the last man."

As the Buzo Tactico attempted to storm Government House the Argentine ⊃

Royal Navy Wessex helicopters ferried mortar crews across the island to ensure they could provide firepower to the troops. (DPL)

Lieutenant Trollope's marines engaged the Argentines with small arms, before withdrawing into the town without loss or injury. This one attack is believed to have killed as many as 32 Argentine marines. In a separate incident another party of marines crippled an Argentine landing craft, hitting it with an 84mm Carl Gustav round as it entered the harbour. The small force of marines at Government House was now fighting against an opposition which heavily outnumbered them in men, equipment, and armour, yet they had crippled the initial advance, albeit for a short time, had taken Argentine prisoners, and had forced the Argentines to bring in their second wave of armour before making a final assault. At 0930hrs the governor of the Falkland Islands, Rex Hunt made the decision to stop firing. He ordered the marines to stop fighting and suddenly it was all over. The marines were flown to Uruguay and then back to the UK.

South Georgia

The invasion came as Royal Marines in Stanley were being relieved. A group headed by Lieutenant Keith Mills was now aboard HMS *Endurance* and in action in South Georgia. Having landed, the 22 commandos

Air defence units armed with Blowpipe launchers were based around San Carlos to intercept incoming Argentine aircraft. (DPL)

2nd Marines Battalion landed and drove into Stanley in their amtracs (armoured, amphibious, tracked personnel carriers) to link up and reinforce the first wave of troops. The leading elements of the 2nd Argentine Marines headed for Government House. On the edge of town, they came under fire from a team of eight Marines commanded by Lieutenant Bill Trollope. They blasted the amtrac at the head of the column with an 84mm Carl Gustav round, then fired two 66mm LAW missiles into it, and for a short time the Argentine armour and the advance was halted.

Members of 45 Commando hitch a ride aboard a tracked BV, which was usually used by the marines in Norway. (DPL)

harassed the Argentines and inflicted as much damage on the enemy as they could. Like the commandos in Stanley, their heaviest weapons were the 84mm Carl Gustav, a shoulder-held anti-tank weapon weighing 36lb, and the smaller and lighter 66mm LAW - a fire-and-forget weapon that could only be used once. They destroyed an Argentine Puma helicopter and when an Argentine corvette arrived offshore and called on the detachment to surrender, Lt Mills and his team opened fire, hitting the vessel several times. The corvette withdrew out of range of the commandos' weapons, then began to pound the detachment with its 100mm gun, and with no options for escape and almost no ammunition left, Lt Mills and his men were forced to surrender. The small teams of Royal Marines operating in Stanley and South Georgia had destroyed an amtrac, a landing craft, a Puma helicopter and had killed or wounded at least 137 Argentines.

When the Falklands was invaded in 1982, Britain's only brigade available for operational deployment was 3 Commando - a formation specially trained in amphibious operations and cold-weather warfare. At the time, the brigade was under the command of Brigadier Julian Thompson. On April 5, a Royal Navy carrier group sailed from Portsmouth and four days later the SS *Canberra* sailed with 3 Commando Brigade and 3 Para aboard.

By the end of April, a task force of warships and civilian vessels requisitioned by the Ministry of Defence had sailed for Ascension Island and the 8,000-mile trip to the Falklands. The task force included two carriers, 23 destroyers and frigates, six submarines, two assault ships and seven landing ships, as well as 12 RFA support ships and more than 50 requisitioned ships. As it sailed south the task force heard that an advance force had recaptured South Georgia on April 25 in an operation codenamed 'Paraquet'. The force, which included M Company of 42 Commando, the SAS, and SBS, had to endure severe weather but their early success lifted morale.

Exclusion Zones

A maritime exclusion zone had been announced by the British on April 12, and at the end of April a total exclusion zone was implemented. By May 1, SAS, SBS and artillery forward observation parties had landed on the Falklands. On the same day, an RAF Vulcan ➲

A Royal Marine sniper team prepare to land ahead of the main force at San Carlos in May 1982. (DPL)

bombed Port Stanley runway. The pressure continued with Sea Harrier raids and on May 2 the Argentine warship the ARA *General Belgrano* was sunk by the submarine HMS *Conqueror*.

Then suddenly, as final plans were made for the landing force, HMS *Sheffield* was sunk by an Exocet missile, and two British Harriers crashed in fog. On May 7, the task force assembled at Ascension. The exclusion zone around the Falklands was extended to 12 miles off the Argentine coast. On May 9 special forces attacked the Argentine spy trawler *Narwhal* then on May 14, the SAS assaulted Pebble Island.

Political options were now running out and on May 18, 1982 the junta rejected British proposals to avoid conflict - the UK government had made a final offer for the withdrawal of Argentine forces from the Falklands. The decision was now made that the task force would land on May 21, at San Carlos, a small settlement 50 miles from Stanley. It offered good landing beaches, but the task force ships would be vulnerable to air attack, as,

Many soldiers suffered with trench foot due to the constant wet and damp conditions they worked in while on the Falklands. (MOD)

critically, the Royal Navy had not been able to win the air war. Pucara ground-attack fighters based on the Falklands and Super Entendard fighters flying from the Argentine mainland threatened the fleet.

Landings begin

Final adjustments to the tactical loading were carried out at sea and Zulu Company moved across to HMS *Intrepid*. On May 20, 45 Commando received their orders and a day later in the early hours of May 21, the men of 40 Commando and 2 Para landed under the Verde and Sussex Mountains by San Carlos settlement, both going ashore in darkness at 0440hrs. Almost an hour later 45 Commando were landed at Ajax Bay and 3 Para a mile west of Port San Carlos. Brigadier Julian Thompson, commander of 3 Commando Brigade expected a counterattack, possibly from troops at Goose Green, and before his force could break out from the bridgehead, he needed to secure the settlement where intelligence reports had confirmed that at least 400 Argentines were based. Thompson had worked with

A Royal Marine marches across the Falklands, the Union flag flying from his backpack. (PH/DPL)

A Royal Marine holds several Argentine prisoners as they wait to be questioned.

take the twin peaks of Two Sisters. The plan tasked X Company to attack the western Sister at 0100hrs, followed two hours later by Y and Z Companies from the northwest to attack the eastern peak. As darkness fell the force made its final preparations and moved off at 2300hrs with Recce Troop leading, followed by Y company, TAC HQ and Z Company - they were just five kilometres from the enemy positions. X Company's attack was delayed, which put back the attack on the eastern peak.

Contact

The leading elements of 45 Commando were within 450 metres of the enemy when suddenly the sound of X Company launching their attack startled the enemy on the eastern peak who realised they were also about to be attacked. The force moved forward using its own artillery and mortar support while X Company cleared positions with Milans. It had been a bitter fight. The group lost four dead and ten wounded. Finally, 45 Commando moved towards Sapper Hill before getting the signal to move into Stanley. After the conflict, the men returned home aboard the *Stromness* and the ➲

the Parachute Regiment before, both on operations and at staff college, and welcomed their involvement. But he was concerned that the units should operate within the brigade as 'one force'. There was no place for rivalry. Not favouring his own units, he gave the first task to the Paras and ordered the 2nd Battalion to Goose Green. Both 45 and 42 Commando, along with 3 Para, were given missions and moved out of San Carlos, but Thompson's old unit, 40 Commando, was ordered to remain in reserve at San Carlos in case the Argentines attempted a counterattack with airborne troops.

The men of 2 Para were to mount the first and bloodiest action of the land war. They marched from Sussex Mountain for the assault on Darwin and Goose Green and after a savage battle secured the latter. At Ajax Bay, 45 Commando - carrying full Bergens and extra ammunition - were ordered to yomp across East Falkland and then launch a night attack on the Argentines defending the Two Sisters feature. At Ajax Bay, the air defence detachment attached to 45 Commando recorded numerous successes as Argentine aircraft swooped in low and fast to attack the task force ships. Marine Wally Walton of Air Defence Troop is credited with destroying a Mirage jet. Marine Alan Steven also shot down a Mirage using the Blowpipe system and Corporal Derek Obbard brought down a Skyhawk at Ajax the day after the landings.

On May 27, 45 Commando moved by landing craft to Port San Carlos and moved up the high ground through 42 Commando's positions. The commandos yomped all day, paused for a meal, then marched on through the night. It was raining and windy and the ground was wet and spongy. The unit continued, with recce deployed ahead and on the flanks with elements of surveillance troops, and secured Douglas settlement on May 28. That night five Royal Marines were killed in an Argentine bombing raid at Ajax Bay. The unit's next objective was Mount Kent, which was to be secured first by 42 Commando who would be lifted by helicopter to their start line. On June 10, 45 Commando had received its orders to

A Sea King airlifts Royal Marine Commandos during operations in the Falklands.

Marines serving with 45 Commando break for food during their yomp across the Falkland Islands in 1982.

Canberra. The names of those who died in the Falklands during 45's operations are carved in stone at the entrance to 45 Commando Group's base at Arbroath in Scotland.

As Goose Green raged, 42 Commando was stood to ready to reinforce 2 Para, but they were not called in. Instead, 42 was tasked to fly forward to Mount Kent. K Company led the advance to Kent with the rest of the force flying in the following night. In wet and freezing conditions, the unit prepared for its main objective Mount Harriet.

Lieutenant Colonel Nick Vaux, the commanding officer of 42 Commando was another very experienced officer and the battle for Mount Harriet was never going to be an easy task. Vaux had codenamed the main feature of Harriet 'Zoya', after his eldest daughter. The feature rose approximately 300 metres and covered the ground leading into Stanley. A second feature called Wall Mountain, from which 42 could observe Harriet, was codenamed 'Tara' after the CO's second daughter. Some of the approaches to Harriet had been mined and heavy machine guns covered the forward slopes, so a frontal assault was ruled out. After a reconnaissance patrol was sent out to evaluate routes, Vaux decided to attack from the southeast, almost to the rear of Harriet. This posed the danger of running into more minefields and being compromised by the moonlight during the yomp to the start line, but Vaux had secured permission to use artillery and mortar fire in a diversionary plan and the Commando made it to the point from which the assault would begin. The commandos used Milan and 66 LAW weapons to clear Argentine positions, and it proved an effective policy. At 0200hrs the attack was launched by K Company and by 1000hrs Harriet had been

Commandos pictured during their march across the island from San Carlos to Port Stanley. (MOD)

45 Commando arrive in Stanley after fighting their way across the Falklands.

secured. It was a hard and long-fought battle in which the unit lost only one marine - possibly because of the use of Milan and 66 LAW to clear enemy positions. The assault had been an outstanding success.

A significant battle of the Falklands conflict which deserves special mention was undertaken by the Mountain and Arctic Warfare (MAW) Cadre who routed the Argentine special forces unit 602 Commando Company at Top Malo. Around 20km northwest of Bluff Cove, Top Malo was an isolated farm, and 19 men of the MAW Cadre surprised the enemy with a rocket attack and a classic right-flanking assault. The attack on May 31 was headed by Captain Rod Boswell, a no-nonsense officer who had dedicated his career to the mountain leader branch of the commandos. A cadre observation post had spotted 16 Argentines of a specialist unit at the location. Boswell's first thought was to call in an air strike, but 42 Commando was about to start a highly dangerous low-level airlift by helicopter across enemy-held ground and the available Harriers were needed for air cover. Other units were resting after events at Goose Green - 45 and 3 Para had just yomped across the islands, and 40 was in the rear to deal with any Argentine counterattack. The presence of an Argentine special forces unit presented a serious threat to 3 Para and 45 Commando and Boswell therefore decided the cadre would have to mount an assault.

The force divided into a seven-man fire section and a 12-man assault group. As they approached the farm it was apparent that only one building, a white-washed stone outbuilding, could contain any force. The others looked dilapidated and deserted. The

A Royal Marine directs Argentine prisoners to a holding area before they are returned to their homeland. (DPL)

fire group was armed with L42 sniper rifles, Armalites and SLRs as well as three M79 grenade launchers and eight 66 LAW rocket launchers. On Boswell's signal - he would fire a green flare - the fire group was to open up with the LAWs and then Boswell, with the assault group, ordered his men to fix bayonets. The fire group quickly destroyed the target house, but the Argentines stormed out, firing back and very quickly two commandos, Sergeant Terry Doyle in the assault group and Sergeant Rocky Stone of the fire group, had been shot and injured. Then Corporal Steve Groves was shot in the chest. Boswell then came face to face with an Argentine who fired his FN. Untouched, Boswell fired back with the Armalite, but it took him four rounds to floor the enemy.

The Argentines surrendered on June 14, 1982 in Port Stanley. The British forces had marched across the island, fighting the enemy on the way to secure victory. The UK lost 255 personnel, and many were wounded. Argentina never released an official figure, but it is estimated that they lost close to 1,000 men. Later, when the entire brigade located itself in and around Stanley, many marines could not believe what they saw. The Argentines had savaged the town, everything had been smashed, set on fire, and destroyed. ●

Lieutenant Colonel Nick Vaux shares a joke with the men of 42 Commando after the war had ended.

THE DESTINATION FOR
MILITARY ENTHUSIASTS
Visit us today and discover all our publications

Classic Military Vehicle - the best-selling publication in the UK dedicated to the coverage of all historic military vehicles.

Britain at War - dedicated to exploring every aspect of the involvement of Britain and her Commonwealth in conflicts from the turn of the 20th century through to the present day.

SIMPLY SCAN THE **QR CODE** OF YOUR FAVOURITE TITLE ABOVE TO FIND OUT MORE!

FREE P&P* when you order
shop.keypublishing.com
Call +44 (0)1780 480404 *(Mon to Fri 9am - 5.30pm GMT)*

389/24

SUBSCRIBE TODAY!

Airforces Monthly is devoted to modern military aircraft and their air arms.

FlyPast is internationally regarded as the magazine for aviation history and heritage.

from our online shop...
/collections/subscriptions

Free 2nd class P&P on all UK & BFPO orders. Overseas charges apply.

FRIENDS AND ALLIES

The US Marines have had a long association with the Royal Marines Commandos. They have served together in Korea, northern Iraq, the Balkans, and Afghanistan as well as training alongside one another in jungle and arctic warfare. This close bond has resulted in many exchange appointments between the two corps with selected instructors from the USMC spending several years at the Commando Training Centre where they have been fully integrated into training teams. Others have served in the mountain and arctic warfare course and other branches of the Royal Marines.

Ironically, the US Marines were formed in 1775 to fight the British at sea and were modelled on the Royal Marines - who had been formed in 1664 to serve at sea. US and British Marines clashed again in 1812, but ever since they have fought on the same side. Since its creation, the USMC has fought across the globe - in the Boxer rebellion in China in 1900, in the Philippines, then in World War Two.

They took part in the famous battle of Iwo Jima. In the post-war years they saw action in Korea, evacuated US nationals from Egypt in 1956, then deployed into Vietnam. In 1979 US Marines took part in the abortive 'Desert One' raid to free US Embassy staff held hostage in Tehran. They joined the invasion force in Grenada in 1984 and then played a major role in the Gulf War. In addition, they have

The US Marines have had a long association with the Royal Marines Commandos. They served together in Korea, northern Iraq, the Balkans, and Afghanistan. (USMC)

Since the early 1970s, when the US pulled out of Vietnam, the soldiers of the British Commando Brigade have carried out regular amphibious exercises with their USMC counterparts. (USMC)

More than any other part of the US's armed forces the Marines symbolise valour, patriotism, and military virtue. (USMC)

The US Marines regularly train in northern Norway with the Royal Marines. (Jack Williams/DPL)

deployed to Bosnia and supported the advance by NATO forces into Kosovo in June 1999.

Since the early 1970s, after the US pulled out of Vietnam, the men of the British Commando Brigade have carried out regular exercises with their USMC counterparts, deploying units to training areas such as Vieques, an island off Puerto Rico which was used by the USMC as a training ground prior to deployment to Vietnam. At that time British converted commando carriers were still in service and entire commando units would exercise seaborne assaults, but as the UK's amphibious asset slipped away in the 1980s and '90s the Royal Marines deployed smaller company groups to train with the US Marines. These partnership exercises focused on tactics and operations in order to give the two forces the opportunity to understand each other's 'standing operational procedures' and weapon systems. Such understanding enhanced joint force operations in areas such as NATO deployment.

Face of the US

More than any other part of the US's armed forces, the Marines symbolise valour, patriotism, and military virtue. They are, in fact, the military face of the USA. The USMC is funded more than any other wing of the US armed forces. Its equipment is constantly being upgraded and the opportunity for those who enlist is as ever global. However, many US Marine NCOs believe that training is now too 'sanitised' and that instructors should be given more training time to shape new recruits who have lived a life in sneakers. A senior USMC instructor said: "Many of the kids that sign up are not mentally tough, they are overweight and out of shape. In the past the 'full metal jacket' approach worked, but not anymore. There are always those who want to be marines, but there are an increasing number of young men and women who see the Corps as a short-term job. It isn't if you join the Corps you need to be here all the way."

Training on the Royal Marine Commando course is three times longer than for US Marines and Americans who have served at Lympstone and passed the commando course are the first to state that it is the hardest infantry test in the world.

The US Marine Corps has its own specialist engineers to clear obstacles and roadside bombers. (USMC)

Osprey V22s have become a key form of strategic transport for the US Marines. (USMC)

The US Marines deployed into Helmand and worked closely alongside the Royal Marines. (USMC)

The US Marines are structured and equipped for projecting American military power onto hostile shores from the sea and for rapid deployment to hot spots around the world. They are unique among fighting forces in that they have their own integrated artillery, armour, aviation, and logistics to support the frontline infantry. The Corps is geographically positioned to operate across two oceans. It covers the Pacific largely from Camp Pendleton in southern California, where the 1st Marine Division is based. The Atlantic is managed by Camp Lejeune, in Jacksonville, North Carolina, where the 2nd Marine Division is based. These camps are huge compared to barracks in the UK - Lejeune, for example, has 61,000 acres of training real estate, miles, and miles of

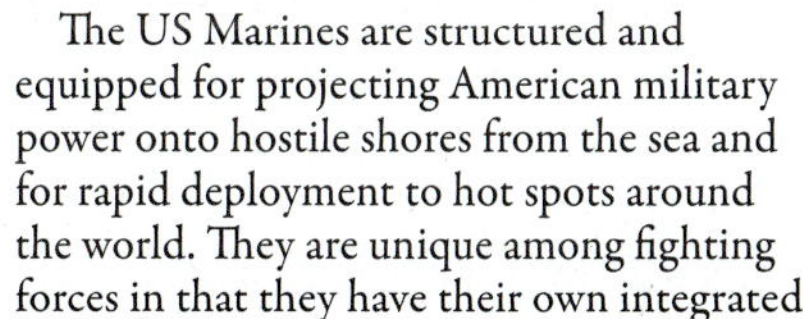
Royal Marines and US Marines prepare to board a Sea King helicopter during exercises in northern Norway. (USMC)

The US Marines have a special assault craft unit – similar to the Royal Marines – but on a much larger scale. (USMC)

beach and more than 45,000 Marines. The force commander can mount seaborne assaults without leaving camp!

2nd Marine Division

While the Royal Marines of 41 Independent Commando fought alongside the 1st Marine Division in Korea, it is the 2nd Marine Division whose sub-units often exercise with today's British commandos. The 2nd Marine Division is the direct descendant of the 2nd Marine Brigade which was activated on July 1, 1936 and saw service in China in 1937 and 1938. As the prospect of war increased and the Marine Corps expanded, division-sized organisations were created. Accordingly, the 2nd Marine Division was officially activated on February 1, 1941 at Camp Elliot, California, dropping its earlier brigade designation. The division was built around the 2nd Marine Regiment which had protected American interests in Latin America and the Caribbean. (The 6th Marine Regiment had established combat records known round the world; the 8th Marine Regiment had seen

Amtracks – armoured amphibious personnel carriers – can transport the marines from ship to the shore. (USMC)

action in Haiti and the division's artillery arm, the 10th Marine Regiment had also been very active.)

Initially, support was provided by service, medical and engineer battalions and transport, tank, signal, chemical and anti-aircraft companies. These supporting organisations have evolved into the six separate battalions within the division. They are Headquarters Battalion, 2nd Assault Amphibious Battalion, 2nd Combat Engineer Battalion, 2nd Light Armoured Infantry Battalion, 2nd Tank Battalion, and the Reconnaissance Battalion. In May 1941, the 6th Marines, and the 2nd Battalion 10th Marines along with support from the 1st Provisional Marine Brigade sailed for Iceland. The Nordic island nation was considered crucial to protection of the seaways between the UK and the US, and Nazi Germany had just invaded Denmark which shared a monarch with Iceland. Similarly, the 2nd Combat Engineer Battalion was sent to Hawaii and helped defend Pearl Harbor during the Japanese attack on December 7, 1941. Immediately after Pearl Harbor, the division deployed along the west coast of the USA to defend it against a possible invasion. In January 1941, a new 2nd Marine Brigade had been formed around the 8th Marines and deployed to American Samoa. By 1942 the Division had been relieved of its defensive duties and began to reorganise for amphibious operations.

In 1942 the 2nd Marine Division saw its earliest action in the first US ground offensive of World War Two - the Guadalcanal ➲

Cliff assault has increasingly become a role within the US Marines and every year one or two marines attend the UK mountain and arctic warfare course, held by the Royal Marines. (USMC)

Light mortars which can be carried by a section and deliver high explosive and smoke are used by US Marine units. (USMC)

campaign. It is this action, fought under the stars of the Southern Cross, which provided the pattern for the five stars in the division emblem.

Post-War

Later, during the Cuban Missile Crisis of 1962, the division was deployed to Guantanamo Bay and the waters off Cuba, remaining there until December of that year. Over the next few years, units of the division were deployed in the Caribbean in response to unrest in the region. In April 1965, elements of the 2nd Division landed in Santa Domingo, Dominican Republic, to protect the lives of American

The US Marines are pioneering new night-vision systems and technology which is changing the battlespace. (USMC)

The US Marines regularly operate with the V22 Osprey. Like the Royal Marines, they focus on night operations using technology to give them a combat advantage over their adversaries. (USMC)

under the Panama Canal Treaty in Operation Just Cause. And in the Gulf War, the entire 2nd Division deployed for the first time since the World War Two. Later, forces from the division deployed on reinforcement operations in Bosnia and supported the advance into Kosovo.

Middle East Deployments

The US Marines worked alongside Royal Marines in Iraq and again in Afghanistan where the 2nd Marine Expeditionary Force deployed to Helmand. In late 2008, an advance party of US Marines from the 24th MEU arrived in Camp Bastion to construct a new base, to be called Camp Leatherneck, as the ISAF troop strengths prepared to soar. US Marines (Task Force 2/7) had trained and mentored the Afghan National Police. In 2009 significant numbers of US Marines arrived in Helmand and were co-located with the UK force at Camp Bastion/Leatherneck. These marines were to play a significant role in Operation

⊃

citizens and aid the evacuation of refugees after a communist-inspired coup. From the end of 1967 until July 1973, the ground defence force of the US Naval Base at Guantanamo Bay was the responsibility of a battalion from the 8th Marines. Later, in October 1979 President Jimmy Carter directed that those forces from the division should again return to the area following Soviet activities in Cuba.

The Marines acted as the ground combat element of the US contribution to the multinational peacekeeping force in Beirut. It was here that the force headquarters was attacked by a suicide bomber in October 1983. In the same year, the 2nd Marines provided the lead element for the US invasion of Grenada.

During the Iran-Iraq War 2nd Division Marines were again in action, serving as the assault force in a raid against an Iranian oil platform. In 1989 elements of the division deployed to Panama to protect US rights

The Royal Netherlands Marines Corps served in Iraq and Afghanistan and regularly train with US and UK forces. (RNLMC)

The V22 Osprey is increasing becoming the workhorse of the US Marines alongside the Chinook and the older CH-53. (USMC)

Moshtarak and would fly into Marja – the heartland of the Taliban - and eject them.

President Obama had agreed to the surge of a further 30,000 troops to support General McChrystal's new 'courageous restraint' strategy'. McChrystal, the overall commander in Afghanistan at the time believed the Coalition needed to win hearts and minds and to avoid killing civilians. His plan was presented simply as 'clear, hold, build and transfer'. Clear was a deliberate action to remove the Taliban; Hold focused on seizing ground; followed by the build phase of infrastructure and governance;

and ultimately the final phase of transferring control to Afghan forces. The US Marines launched the main thrust of the offensive, focusing on Marjah, an insurgent and drug-smuggling stronghold situated to the southwest and faced fierce figting, but secured the area and defeated the enemy. The last US Marines to withdraw from Helmand province flew home to San Diego in 2014, ending five years of combat in the deadliest area of Helmand. The USMC initially sent a brigade of 9,000 to support British forces. Sending the Marines to Helmand instead of neighbouring Kandahar,

where the US Army was struggling to secure the second-largest city in Afghanistan and the spiritual birthplace of the Taliban, was a controversial decision.

The brigade demonstrated the utility of its larger footprint of ground troops when it seized the farm town of Nawa in summer 2009. Within three months, residents began returning to the deserted area. Market stalls reopened, the district governor was on the job and Taliban checkpoints and roadside bombs disappeared. Nawa became safe enough for marines to routinely walk downtown without their body

A wounded US Marine is airlifted to a field hospital in Afghanistan during operations in Helmand. (USMC)

armour. But as the years passed politicians opted to drawdown and pull out leaving the Afghan National Army to take charge – they collapsed in the face of the Taliban.

The Royal Netherlands Marine Corps

Britain's Royal Marine Commandos and the Royal Netherlands Marine Corps (RNLMC) have worked together for several decades, developing a unique partnership. The first liaison between the two forces took place in 1965 when a company of

The US Marines operate a number of specialist sniper teams, and many attend the Royal Marines' prestigious sniper course. (USMC)

Dutch Marines came to the UK to exercise with 43 Commando RM. In 1972 both formations deployed on winter warfare training to Norway. This was followed by further joint ventures before the partnership was made official in 1973. On May 9 of that year the defence ministers of the UK and the Netherlands signed a memorandum of understanding to formalise the establishment of closer military cooperation and Whisky Company of the RNLMC joined 45 Commando RM at Arbroath in Scotland.

The Dutch company remained under 45's operational control at Condor barracks for many years as the UK/NL project developed. The Netherlands Marines were totally integrated into the commando group as the concept of a joint amphibious landing force matured. By the late 1970s the 'cloggies' as they were affectionately known were exercising all over the world with the Royal Marines and in 1979 a much larger contribution to the UK/NL Landing Force was made when the battalion-sized 1st Amphibious Combat Group was assigned to operate as part of 3 Commando Brigade on NATO operations.

It was in June 1977 that the Royal Netherlands Marine Corps mounted its most overt operation: the unit's anti-terrorist specialists were called in to resolve a hijack situation in which armed South Moluccans had seized a train and taken 80 passengers hostage. The train, a commuter service on its way between Rotterdam and Groningen in northern Holland, had been hijacked on May 23 and halted at De Pont.

The terrorists wanted the Dutch government to exert pressure on the Indonesian government to grant independence to South Molucca. They demanded that a Boeing 747 be made available at Amsterdam's Schiphol airport and to demonstrate their violent intent they shot dead the train driver and threw his body onto the rails. After 19 days of siege negotiation the authorities handed over control of the incident to the Dutch Marines.

On June 11, seconds before the Marines stormed the train, a pair of Dutch Air Force F-104 Starfighters screamed in low and fast to confuse the hijackers. As they peeled away, charges on the carriage doors were detonated ➲

US Marines in Helmand where they served in Garmsir and crippled Taliban operations. (USMC)

The US Marines are continually testing new weapons and equipment. (USMC)

The RNLMC train in similar way to the Royal Marines – operating in small teams which strike from the sea by boat or helicopter. (RNLMC)

and the assault teams moved in. In total six hijackers were killed and seven arrested. Sadly, two passengers also died.

In 1991 a substantial reorganisation of the RNLMC resulted in all operational units being incorporated into what is called the Group of Operational Units Marines (GOUM) which enhanced the forces' ability to support the UK/NL landing force and resulted in the commander of the GOUM being made deputy commander of the joint amphibious force. The GOUM consists of four infantry battalions. One of these is a reserve battalion - of which the sub-units are stationed in the Dutch Antilles and Aruba on a permanent basis while two operational infantry battalions are based in the Netherlands (1st and 2nd Marine Battalions). In 1991, just a year after the Gulf War, the many years of joint training and exercises came to fruition when the UK/NL force had its first joint operational deployment to northern Iraq during Operation Safe Haven - a humanitarian mission to provide relief and protection for thousands of Kurds fleeing Iraq. Then, in 1992 and 1993 the Dutch Marines deployed three battalions

A US Marine manning a heavy machine gun and wearing the corps' new digital camouflage clothing. (USMC)

to Cambodia on United Nations duty. At the end of 1994 they took part in a UN mission to Haiti which was followed in 1995 by providing a rapid reaction force to support UNPROFOR (the United Nations Protection Force) in Bosnia. Later, a heavy mortar battery was deployed with IFOR/SFOR (Implementation Force/Stabilisation Force) in Bosnia. RNLMC manpower currently stands at just over 3,000 and the Marine Corps' headquarters is located in the centre of Rotterdam. A recruit's training takes approximately 25 weeks, and the centre runs six courses per year. It is here that various specialist training also takes place, such as sniper and mortar work.

Additional parachuting, commando and special forces training is undertaken elsewhere in the Netherlands, as well as overseas where jungle warfare, combat skiing and climbing courses are held. Today, the Dutch Marines are adopting technology in the same manner as the Royal Marines, they have high-readiness units poised to deploy in support of the country's defence policy and send personnel to attend the mountain and arctic warfare leaders course run by the Royal Marines. ●

Heavy mortar fire at night is deployed by the US Marines in support of their infantry. (USMC)

When the first Royal Marine Commandos deployed to Northern Ireland in September 1969, few could have predicted that they would be the advance party for the corps' longest operational campaign. (DPL)

THE LONGEST WAR

When the first Royal Marine Commandos deployed to Northern Ireland in September 1969, few could have predicted that they would be the advance party for the corps' longest operational campaign and bear witness to some of the most sickening terrorist violence of the 20th century. Furthermore, no one could have forecast that more than three decades later the green berets of 3 Commando Brigade would still be serving in the province as peace initiatives seemed to come and go while bitterness and deep-seated religious rivalry continued to split the communities.

British troops were rushed to the province on an emergency tour in 1969 to defuse confrontation between Protestant and Catholic communities. Their aim was to create a climate of security. At this point, through the fog of a thousand myths and the propaganda of the Republican press machine, it is important to remember the mission of the British Army units and the Royal Marines who first deployed to Ulster was to protect the Catholic community. In five days of relentless riots that raged from Londonderry to Belfast seven people had been killed and 750 injured. More than 1,500 Catholic families had been burnt out of their homes while 315 Protestants lost theirs.

Trouble had flared throughout the 1960s as Protestant extremists hit back at Nationalists following the failure of an Irish Republican

Army (IRA) campaign that took place between 1956 and 1962. The campaign cost the lives of six members of the Royal Ulster Constabulary (RUC) and 11 B Specials. In retaliation the Protestant Ulster Volunteer Force (UVF) shot dead a Catholic on April 27, 1966. Another victim was shot in June. A period of calm returned for about two years, but then in 1968 there was more civil unrest when a Northern Ireland civil rights march, formed by Catholics from across the social classes, paraded through Londonderry on October 5, 1968. The demonstration had been banned by the home affairs minister and when it went ahead police units moved in with batons; 75people were injured. Throughout 1969 tension increased as the situation deteriorated. The British Army's senior officer, Lieutenant General Sir Ian Freeland had only 2,500 troops based in Ulster and had made contingency plans to deploy them to guard government buildings. By July, the government had approved the use of CS ➲

A Royal Marine mobile patrol passes a Loyalist housing estate on the edge of West Belfast which was largely dominated by the Republican community. (DPL)

In September 41 Commando arrived in Belfast as part of Operation Banner. Their task was to protect the Catholic community from extremist Protestant attacks. (DPL)

A Royal Marine foot patrol in West Belfast chats to a local man about his concerns in the area. (DPL)

request of the Northern Ireland government who sought military assistance following months of sectarian violence. In September, 41 Commando arrived in Belfast as part of Operation Banner. Their task was to protect the Catholic community from extremist Protestant attacks and the commandos were welcomed with smiling faces, applause and offers of tea and cakes whenever they entered a Republican estate. During its two-month emergency tour 41 Commando suffered seven casualties. Across the province there had been more than 70 shootings, as well as 10 bombs, and an RUC officer and 10 civilians killed. Two Republican terrorists had died, and 14 weapons were recovered. Although 41 Commando had only witnessed a small fragment of this, it had been a busy tour.

Heightened tensions

In June 1970, 45 Commando RM arrived in Belfast and adopted tactics they had last used in Aden and stripped their Land Rovers down - canvas roofs and doors removed - to give them greater visibility and the flexibility to deploy from the vehicle at speed in pursuit of suspects. The principle was obviously a wise one because within months a wide range of other units followed suit. However, stripped-down Land Rovers were only practical until they faced a crowd of brick-throwing rioters.

gas by the Royal Ulster Constabulary and on August 12 it was deployed for the first time in the UK as riots flared in the Bogside area of Londonderry.

On August 13, the first troops were sent to reinforce the police in Londonderry. The following day they were deployed to the Bogside after an exhausted 3,200-strong RUC requested military assistance. Then on day four ten civilians were killed, 145 were injured and four policemen were wounded in gun battles. The troops had been sent in by the Labour Prime Minister Harold Wilson at the

Commandos armed with the SLR rifle board a Lynx helicopter at Bessbrook military base in the mid 1970s. (DPL)

Shortly after its arrival, 45 Commando was tasked, along with the 1st Battalion the King's Own Scottish Borderers and the 1st Battalion the Royal Scots, to keep protesting Nationalists away from marching Orangemen. 45 Commando RM was responsible for a district of Belfast that included the Crumlin Road which had the Republican Ardoyne area to the north and the Protestant Shankhill to the south. On June 26, eight Orange lodge bands marched, totalling some 500 people in the parade with a further 2,500 following and by early evening a crowd of more than 200 Nationalist youths had begun stoning elements of Support Company who had used a 3-tonner lorry and a Land Rover to block a side street where the mob was advancing. Everything from house bricks to ball-bearings, bottles, marbles, coins, and cans was thrown at the marines and almost every man received some sort of injury. The troop officer, a young lieutenant, was hit straight in the face with a brick. While his wounds were being dressed the troop sergeant took command. A much larger crowd of approximately 2,000 Nationalists was held back by the main force of 45 Commando while the RUC prevented 3,500 Orangemen from attacking the Catholics. Throughout the night the rioting continued but at dawn the crowds disappeared home. Later that morning confrontation sparked across Belfast with

Commandos board a Wessex helicopter at Bessbrook in South Armagh, an area known as 'Bandit Country' as a direct result of the number of shootings. (DPL)

hospitals reporting more than 200 injured. 45 Commando's patch was quiet until mid-afternoon when another Orange march sparked an IRA sniper attack in the Ardoyne in which a Protestant civilian was killed.

By early evening, the trouble had been quelled by 45 Commando, but later that summer's night alcohol fuelled the rioters' bravado, and they were back on the streets. A stolen bus was driven into a pub and within ➲

HRH the Duke of Edinburgh, who was the captain general of the corps, visits the Royal Marines in Northern Ireland. (DPL)

Marine Pete Russell, who served in the province during the early '70s, said he found Ulster stressful, he recalled: "My section commander was an old sweat and before we got on the ground, he told us not to take any shit. It was a weird sensation being on the streets for the first time, trying to watch where you were walking while at the same time looking at every spot you thought could be used by a sniper. I don't mind telling you I was delighted when that first patrol was over, and we returned to base."

On March 24, 1972 Westminster dissolved the Stormont parliament and took direct control of Northern Ireland. It was a controversial decision which Republicans refused to accept and resulted in 'no-go' zones being established in many hardline areas as they attempted to establish their own communities in protest at the British government's action. In June, 40 Commando RM arrived for its first tour in Ulster and was to witness some of worst days of violence in the province. Protestant marches reached minutes an angry crowd of more than 150 had gathered. Just one troop of Marines ploughed in to restore order, donning respirators, and using tear gas to push the crowd back while at the same time sending in snatch squads to arrest seven of the ringleaders. Then a gunman fired several rounds, possibly from an Armalite, one of which cut through Marine Terry Glover's riot shield, struck his belt, and lodged itself in the cleaning kit box for his SLR. The rioting continued throughout the night with cars set on fire and houses torched, but the following day normality returned, and the Butler Street riots were over - at least as far as 45 was concerned. Throughout the 72-hour period the Commando had stayed on the street, taking turns to grab a few hours' sleep.

Operation Demetrius

By the mid-1970s mobs were out on the streets every night, stoning soldiers, torching buildings, hi-jacking buses and generally destroying the infrastructure and economic fabric of Ulster. This high level of public disorder, combined with increased terrorist attacks against the security forces, resulted in the government introducing internment on Monday August 9. In support of the internment a massive operation named Operation Demetrius was mounted to round up the 'alleged known players' and in the early hours battalions across Northern Ireland were given allocated areas in which they were to 'lift' suspects.

At this time 45 Commando RM was on standby as the 'Spearhead' battalion, ready to deploy on operations anywhere in the world but were back in Northern Ireland to assist in 'Demetrius' and arrived on August 10 for a three-week stint. Reaction to internment was fierce and crowds gathered to protest throughout the Nationalist areas. Barricades were erected and as 45 moved in to clear them, petrol bombs rained down. Later that year 45 Commando RM returned, this time for a four-month tour of Belfast, arriving on October 17. Just a week later 42 Commando RM also arrived in the province and deployed in Armagh and Dungannon. Both units sustained casualties but no fatal injuries. Between 1970 and 1974, 45 Commando was to serve five tours in Ulster, one of them a short emergency tour. Former

An Army Air Corps Lynx helicopter lifts off with Royal Marines onboard for an operation in South Armagh. (DPL)

The rioting in Belfast became intense in the late 1970s with the Royal Marines forming snatch squads to detain the ringleaders. (DPL)

their peak and the creation of Catholic 'no-go' areas forced a major military operation. By the middle of 1972 'no-go' zones had spread across West Belfast and Londonderry. The violence increased as gunmen sought refuge from the security forces in the Nationalist estates where they thought they would be free from capture. After Bloody Friday, July 21, when bombs shattered Belfast and left nine people dead, a plan was drawn up to clear the no-go areas and restore law and order in the province. Codenamed Operation Motorman, the operation took place in July 1972 and was the largest to be mounted by the British Army since Suez. It involved 21,000 troops from 27 different units and included four Centurion tanks, which were fitted with bulldozer blades to clear the barricades. These tanks were known as AVREs (Armoured Vehicle Royal Engineers) and were deployed from landing craft on the River Foyle.

Hundreds of armoured vehicles supported the operation which began before dawn on July 31. All three units, 45, 40, and 42 Commandos took part in the Belfast phase of 'Motorman'. 42 moved into Ligoneil and 40 into the New Lodge. The operation attracted massive television coverage as Saladin and Saracen armoured personnel carriers drove through the streets of Republican estates, the convoy smashing down the Nationalists' checkpoints. The no-go barriers were destroyed in the first six hours of the operation which took 24 hours to complete.

No Let Up

In the summer of 1972, 40 Commando deployed to North Belfast in an area which included the hard-line Republican community of Unity Flats and the New Lodge. The Commando was led by Lieutenant Colonel John Mottram, a robust officer who led from the front and was respected by all his men. This was perhaps one of the hardest tours faced by a Commando. Almost every day

In the early 1980s the commandos did not wear badges on their smocks and avoided wearing rank insignia so that locals who might be 'spotting' for the IRA could not tell who was in charge. (DPL)

As the attacks increased, armoured Land Rovers were introduced to safeguard soldiers from rocket and home-made grenade attacks. (DPL)

The RAF Puma helicopter was the fastest rotary platform available and was deployed to South Armagh along with the Chinook. (DPL)

Every time the police, then called the RUC deployed, the military had to provide an escort for them. In the main the RUC had superior equipment to the army. (DPL)

The commandos were able to cripple IRA smuggling operations with small boat patrols on the border waterways. (DPL)

In the true style of the corps the commandos were, as in previous campaigns, keen to introduce new tactics to make their job more efficient. Assault engineers formed special search parties because they had all the necessary kit and in 1974 Marines of 45 Commando introduced the first 'Eagle flights' across the notorious bandit area on the border between Ulster and Eire. Heliborne sections of Marines flew across designated areas, landing at regular intervals to mount vehicle checkpoints. This gave 45 Commando the advantage of surprise in their pursuit of terrorists. Other units adopted the procedure, and it became a successful tactic until the IRA obtained surface-to-air missiles.

Car bombs and IEDs

At the height of the car bomb threat, disposal teams were stretched to the limits dealing with suspect devices across the province.

In 1974 two Royal Marines from 45 Commando RM were killed during the unit's tour in South Armagh. The men, Corporal Dennis Leach, aged 24, and Marine Michael Southern, 19, died when they were blown up by

there were gun battles and two months into the operation the CO was given the additional responsibility of commanding 1 Royal Scots and two companies of 42 Commando as well as his own unit for 'Motorman'. It was during this tour that the first Royal Marine Commando to be killed on active service in Ulster lost his life - Marine Lennard Allen. Later during the same tour, a second Marine from 40 Commando RM, Marine Anthony David, was killed. A further 17 Marines were injured, some of them seriously. For clarity, the first soldier to be killed in Ulster was Gunner Robert Curtis who was shot by an IRA gunman as he patrolled the New Lodge on February 6, 1971.

As the years passed many Marines and senior officers became frustrated with the situation in the province. A retired officer who served with 42 and 45 Commando on numerous tours summed up his feelings about Ulster with disgust. He said: "The problem is the IRA were at war with us, but we were not allowed to be at war with them. There was never any resolve to move ahead. The mission was always containment."

A Royal Marine serving with 45 Commando pictured during a search operation at a border town in Fermanagh. (DPL)

Marine Commandos take a moment's rest during disturbances in West Belfast. (DPL)

a radio-controlled IRA bomb which had been buried near their position at Drummuckavall.

At Condor in Arbroath, the home of 45 Commando, two roads on the married quarters estate were named after them - Leach Close and Southern Close. In 1976, 40 Commando RM deployed to South Armagh. Terrorist attacks in the border region had soared and it had been some time since a unit sent to the area had not sustained a fatal casualty. On August 17, 1976, the Marines of 40 Commando RM arrived at Belfast harbour on a landing ship and drove to Bessbrook Mill base in South Armagh. They arrived in a convoy of lorries escorted by Land Rovers of 3 Para - the battalion they were replacing. From Bessbrook companies were flown forward to various locations - these were smaller patrol bases at sites including Crossmaglen, Forkhill, and Newry where, with the gunners of 145 Commando Battery of 29 Commando RA and elements of 40 Commando's Support Company they were based at Newry RUC station.

The unit's first incident occurred within one minute of their taking over the area with a report of an incendiary bomb in a shop at Warrenpoint. The Battery and

Royal Marines and paratroopers are pictured in a joint operation on the border in South Armagh. (DPL)

The commandos mounted 'snap' vehicle check points across their area of operation to stop the terrorists moving guns around. (DPL)

Loyalist parades often erupted into violence in the evening forcing commandos and other units to be on standby. (DPL)

40 Commando's mortar troop were co-located at Newry RUC station. Their quick reaction force and bomb disposal team quickly dealt with the incident - the first of many. Newry became a busy patch with regular hijackings and shootings.

The Commando's Alpha Company, commanded by Major Colin Howgill, had a very difficult task. It was based in Crossmaglen, the heartland of the Nationalist community which has seen more British soldiers killed by the IRA than any other area of Northern Ireland. The IRA made great use of IEDs (improvised explosive devices) because they provided maximum impact and maximum chance of escape for the Active Service Unit (ASU) involved. Crossmaglen had seen IEDs on roads, culverts, and farm gates. In fact, just before the unit's arrival the IRA had packed a bike with explosives and detonated it just off the main square in Crossmaglen as a patrol from 3 Para passed and Private James Borucki was killed. Later, a sangar was erected on the corner of the square and named in his memory. Borucki Sangar remained a key observation

The commandos chatted to innocent civilians to make sure they were happy and dominated South Armagh making it difficult for illegal organisations to operate (DPL)

Riot training became more intense with special flame proof uniforms being issued. (DPL)

tower in Crossmaglen until July 30, 2000 when work started to dismantle it as part of the Good Friday peace agreement.

Before the Royal Marine Commandos deployed to Ulster in 1976 the IRA propaganda machine announced that it would kill ten Marines. Despite mounting two attempts in separate mortar attacks, it failed. Then on October 17, 1981 the IRA attempted to murder the commandant general of the corps, Lieutenant General Sir Stuart Pringle in a car bomb attack outside his home. The commandant general suffered serious injuries and lost a leg, but his cheerful spirit and determination was an inspiration to the corps and by early 1982 he was back at work in his Whitehall office.

In 1989 the IRA was still looking for a major attack on the corps and on September 22, it struck at the Royal Marine barracks at Deal in Kent, killing 11 band musicians. While Northern Ireland remains the longest campaign for the Royal Marines and all other British military units operating there, it is perhaps the only one where progress has been limited by political indecision and more recently 'political correctness'. By 2000 the Royal Marines had recorded 39 tours of the province over almost 14 years worth of duty. Fourteen Marines had lost their lives in Ulster and ninety-four had been injured, many of them seriously. As the Royal Marines and the British Army enter the 21st century 40 Commando recorded the corps' 40th tour of duty when it was deployed to Northern Ireland as a Brigade reserve for the period of the marching season and in particular the Drumcree march in 2000.

The troubles ended with the Good Friday Agreement of 1998. The final word on Northern Ireland must go to those on the front line. A young Marine who deployed in 2000 on his first tour of duty said: "The Republican hate was deep; generations had learnt to despise each other many did not want the violence to end. The Good Friday deal pushed it under ground. For the veterans there is unfinished business – only the young can prevent more conflict." ●

As the Good Friday peace deal approached troops supported the police but gradually pulled back from the streets. (DPL)

THE COMMANDO FORCE

Commando operations inherently require a maritime element and in the late 1990s a new dedicated helicopter carrier and an assault ship were seen as platforms that would allow a large amphibious task force to develop, which could be at sea ready to deploy a commando battlegroup to an area of conflict within hours or days. They were an attractive asset for any government, particularly in a global environment where the next flashpoint is often hard to predict.

At the time doctrine to support commando operations portrayed a force with the freedom to loiter off a coast, withdraw or concentrate in international waters without violating frontiers, and be used as a potent political tool. The mere departure of amphibious forces from their home base was seen as a demonstration of political intent. In addition, the force could put to sea amid much publicity or sail out without statement. Once in theatre, amphibious forces can be held poised to intervene while political

HMS *Ocean*-ordered as a new dedicated helicopter carrier - is seen deployed with US and French warships in the Mediterranean. (DPL)

alternatives to military action are explored; their sheer presence can exert favourable pressure on negotiations. This was without question a powerful military tool in the 1970s and through to the later 1990s – although technology would later impact on this concept.

During the 1960s and '70s, the Commando Brigade often found itself diverting a unit aboard a carrier or assault ship away from an exercise to potential operational deployment, such as Cyprus in 1974. At one point the Royal Navy fielded two commando ships – converted aircraft carriers - and two assault ships.

The full potential of a floating expeditionary force able to remain at sea, on-call, ready to support political intent was probably never grasped by the Ministry of Defence; neither was it needed. In the 1970s ministers were preoccupied with the problems of Northern Ireland and with ensuring that British forces were prepared for a Soviet assault both across Europe and through northern Norway. It was perhaps the 'threatening intent' that amphibious commando forces can deliver that

Commando operations inherently require a maritime force to allow it to mount operations and provide the ability to project power. (DPL)

The assault ships allow amphibious forces to get ashore from landing craft and helicopters in often remote areas. (DPL)

Inside the helicopter carrier HMS *Ocean*, a lift was fitted to raise helicopters and bring commandos to the flight deck. (MOD)

helped persuade politicians to secure the amphibious capability of the commandos in the government's Strategic Defence Review of 1999, which fundamentally influenced the future of the Royal Marines Commandos. Never before in their history had the Royal Marines been assigned so much new equipment and resources to ensure that the amphibious role was retained. New assault ships were confirmed, and a specialist helicopter carrier sought to deliver greater capability to the commando force.

Applying a concept known as the Amphibious Ready Group (ARG) a commando battlegroup could now deploy aboard HMS *Ocean*, the new helicopter carrier, or one of the new assault ships and head to an area of potential crisis identified by intelligence staff at the Permanent Joint Headquarters (PJHQ). The ARG could then wait in international waters. The force provided amphibious elements based around a commando group with supporting joint assets. These could include RAF Chinook helicopters, specialist army units and RAF Harrier GR7s, which could join the force aboard an aircraft carrier. The doctrine allowed the ARG to be deployed as far forward as possible, while capable of meeting a wide range of warfighting and non-warfighting tasks. The ARG elevated the commando force to the same expeditionary status as their cousins in the US Marines. It was seen, at the time, as cost effective and delivered an important statement of UK military capability. During its period afloat, potentially a three-month operation, the embarked commando battlegroup could deploy ashore to exercise with host nations of the NATO alliance. The assault ships provided a floating dock, landing craft to ferry stores ashore, and a flight deck for several helicopters while the helicopter carrier had enough capacity to fly almost half a commando unit ashore in one sortie. This was commando operations at scale and the amphibious fleet was vulnerable – it needed protection from air-defence destroyers, anti-submarine frigates and submarines. HMS *Ocean* was seen as the spearhead of the naval force, having flown the commandos ashore the ship's helicopters could ferry artillery guns, engineering assets and help maintain the force ashore.

Assault Ships

The new assault ships HMS *Albion* and HMS *Bulwark* together with HMS *Ocean* and several Bay-class landing ships secured the commando's future. There was no question that future operations would see the ARG making a major contribution. HMS *Ocean* was commissioned into the Royal Navy in 1998 and after training off northern Norway and Scotland in 2000 the helicopter carrier deployed for the first time in routine exercises in the Mediterranean. HMS *Ocean* - with 42 Commando RM, artillery and engineering assets embarked - was scheduled to take part in a series of NATO amphibious exercises while senior commanders were also aware that they could be pulled away at any point to react to any crisis situation, including a reinforcement of the Balkans. Within two months of the carrier's departure from her base port at Plymouth in Devon the ARG was redirected by the Permanent Joint Headquarters to potentially deploy to Sierra Leone in west Africa.

Sierra Leone had been the focus of conflict for a number of years and Royal Marines from the Fleet Standby Rifle Troop (FSRT) – a small high readiness force - had been in Freetown a year earlier to assist in security on a deployment named Operation Resilient. The FSRT teams from 45 Commando RM had flown in with Brigadier David Richards, the then head of the Joint Headquarters at Northwood. They deployed into Freetown from a warship after the British Embassy had been evacuated following increased violence in late 1998 as the Revolutionary United Front (RUF) moved into Freetown. The force, consisting of just 22 marines, supported by elements of 539 Assault Squadron and a Navy Lynx helicopter, secured the embassy and delivered medical supplies after rebels left hundreds of mutilated victims in the capital, hacking off the limbs of men, women, and children.

With helicopters and landing craft the assault force can land troops almost anywhere from the Arctic to the jungle, (DPL)

The marines used vehicles from the British High Commission and worked in liaison with Nigerian troops assigned to the United Nations operation. In early 1999 the FSRT teams pulled out, although Sierra Leone remained most definitely listed as an 'area of interest' by the planning teams at the Permanent Joint Headquarters. By May 2000 the British High Commissioner in Freetown, Alan Jones, warned that the situation in the capital had deteriorated and advised London that an evacuation of British nationals should not be delayed.

Once the decision had been made to evacuate British Nationals, military planners sent in a battalion of paratroopers for what was seen as a three-day mission. The Parachute Regiment arrived on May 8 and seized the airport, in what was named Operation Palliser, and quickly airlifted 500 out of the country. Having dealt with the initial task the Paras were then directed to mount a security operation around the capital Freetown and restore public confidence as rebel gangs continued to operate and fears grew that the rebel RUF was preparing to mount an attack on Freetown.

Aboard HMS *Ocean* the embarked force was spearheaded by 42 Commando RM and included elements of 29 Commando Royal Artillery and engineer support from 59 Independent Commando Squadron Royal Engineers. In addition, the force included Sea King helicopters and the full suite of logistics support available from stores on board the carrier and from the flotilla of naval support ships and warships escorting her. In the first week of May the carrier docked at Marseilles for a planned programme of cross-training with French forces but within days the visit had been abandoned and HMS *Ocean* put to sea. Her commander, Captain Lidbetter had received an 'eyes only' signal regarding the growing unrest in Sierra Leone and was directed to 'stand off' the Ivory Coast. Back in London the Defence Secretary Geoff Hoon approved plans to divert the aircraft carrier HMS *Illustrious* to the area. At the time, ➲

The alternative to landing craft was a system called 'mexifloats' which took longer to deploy and were often carried by support ships. (DPL)

The two assault ships, HMS *Albion* and HMS *Bulwark* were identical and could help move almost all of the commando brigade. (MOD)

Illustrious was off Lisbon and heading back to the UK. At Gibraltar the carrier was joined by the Type 22 frigate HMS *Chatham* which had men from 148 Forward Observation Battery of 29 Commando RA aboard as well as boats from 539 Assault Squadron, which had been flown out to 'the Rock'. More Royal Marines from the Fleet Standby Rifle Troop, now sustained by Comancchio Group, deployed aboard the Type 23 frigate HMS *Argyll* (Royal Marine Protection Party 3) to support the operation.

Joint Rapid Reaction Force

Back in 1996 the Joint Rapid Reaction Force (initially the Joint Rapid Deployment Force) had been formed. It included both 3 Commando Brigade and the then 5 Airborne Brigade to provide a light battalion for immediate readiness on alternate periods of standby. A host of additional specialist units were also assigned to the force to be used in a 'mission requirement' role. Now in west Africa, the two units were to take part in a peace support operation that would demonstrate for

The new assault ships secured the future of the commandos' amphibious capability. (MOD)

HMS *Ocean* was built with wide corridors and walkways to accommodate the marines' equipment. (MOD)

the first time the full benefit of joint operations working within the JRRF. The Kosovo deployment by the 1st Battalion Parachute Regiment in June 1999 had demonstrated RAF and British Army cooperation, but Sierra Leone was truly tri-service. As HMS *Ocean* sailed for the west African coast, RAF C-130 aircraft were mounting an evacuation in Sierra Leone with the Paras and additional naval units were heading for the region.

HMS *Ocean* and HMS *Illustrious* arrived off the Ivory Coast to establish a maritime task group. This group was able to provide a commando battlegroup from 42 Commando to support the Paras ashore, to launch combat air patrols by Harriers aboard the carrier, and to act as a secure environment for operational briefings. The source of the problem in Sierra Leone was focused on the rebels of the RUF and rogue gangs, namely a group called the West Side Boys, armed and high on drugs who had been 'at war' with President Kabbah's government forces for several years. Now as the Paras had overseen the evacuation and established security the marines were sent into relieve them.

Within days of arriving the marines deployed inflatable raiding craft and mounted river patrols on the key waterway separating Freetown from the airport at Lungi. The marine coxwains had been ordered to remove their commando flashes, worn on the shoulder of Combat 95 uniform, so that the media would not be alerted to the fact that the commando group was ashore. As the Paras pulled out, 42 Commando officially rolled into Freetown. The operation was more of a media event than a tactical arrival, as many of the commando ➥

Both assault ships could carry hovercraft which were deployed in Norway and later carried to the Middle Est and used in the raid on the Al Faw Peninsula. (MOD)

The assault ships and helicopter carrier could land a force in an area such as the Brunei jungle, sustain it, and provide a rear headquarters. (MOD)

group had already been working with the Paras - either alongside them collating intelligence in preparation for the handover or preparing accommodation and identifying resources for the unit.

The arrival of the commando force was a show of military might and on May 24 the 105mm light guns of 8 Battery 29 Commando RA were flown ashore and positioned at Petify Junction and Lungi airport. WMIK (Weapon Mounted Installation Kit) Land Rovers provided a highly visible presence on the streets while, more importantly, ensuring a significant level of firepower with .50 mounted machine guns and GPMG.

Just days before 42 Commando took over, three British officers and a New Zealander, who had been held by rebel forces, escaped from their captors - one of them was a Royal Marine, Major Philip Ashby who telephoned his wife from the UN base where they were held and she alerted PJHQ. Then the four made their escape,

Maritime exercises and operations require advance surveillance which was delivered by Brigade Patrol Troop. (DPL)

trekking 40 miles through the bush at night to a rendezvous with an RAF Chinook.

The deployment into Sierra Leone had been a pertinent reminder to ministers of the 'on-call' capability of the newly formed ARG, allowing the Commando Brigade to demonstrate its inherent flexibility to be ready for operations. As 42 Commando returned to the UK, Taunton-based 40 Commando was preparing for yet another tour of duty in Northern Ireland. As peace seemed to evaporate across the Province, the unrest at Drumcree and increased violence in Belfast saw the commandos back on the streets in June 2000. The unit's tour saw Support Company and its intelligence cell deployed in Belfast and other elements of 40 tasked to support operations at Drumcree. It was the last time the Royal Marines would patrol the streets of Ulster.

NATO's northern flank is another example of a region where helicopters could deliver troops in the Arctic. (MOD)

The intervention by the Royal Marines in Sierra Leone was managed to show the rebels the military power that a UK force could deliver if they attempted to overthrow the government. (DPL)

During the Sierra Leone operation, artillery was ferried ashore in daylight to make sure that groups such as the West Side Boys were able to see the UK capability. (MOD)

fate since the deployment of KFOR in the region in June 1999.

The most significant role of the helicopter carrier and its integrated commando force took place in 2003 when in southern Iraq – just a couple of years after the UK sent troops into Afghanistan. The assault on the Al-Faw Peninsula in southern Iraq was a complex amphibious operation – launched from

Kosovo and Iraq

At the turn of the millennium, the commandos found themselves in Kosovo, operating as part of the Multi-National Brigade as 45 Commando deployed on peace support operations in the wake of NATO's intervention to protect Albanians from ethnic cleansing. NATO has been equally committed to protecting the ethnic Serbs from a similar

HMS *Ocean* could carry most types of support helicopter with the Sea King, Chinook, and Merlin often being embarked. (MOD)

As the Royal Marine Commandos landed in Sierra Leone they drove through the centre of Freetown – again making sure the civilian population could be reassured and the rebels warned. (MOD)

An RAF Chinok ferried a 105mm light gun ashore in Freetown as the marines mounted an amphibious landing. (MOD)

A view of the helicopter deck aboard HMS *Ocean* during the night time raid into the Al Faw peninsula. (MOD)

bases on land in Kuwait and from HMS *Ark Royal* and HMS *Ocean* in the northern Gulf. It led to the collapse of the Iraqi Army, the fall of the country's second city, and prevented an ecological catastrophe. The Al-Faw peninsula – a flat, largely featureless area larger than

The Royal Marines mounted the raid into Iraq's Al Faw peninsula aboard UK and US Marines helicopters. (DPL)

The Royal Navy's Sea King helicopters worked around the clock to deliver troops ashore and sustain them during the Al Faw operation. (DPL)

Norfolk – was home to the bulk of Iraq's oil fields and infrastructure, as well as the country's only deep-water port, Umm Qasr.

The rapid capture of the peninsula, defended by the Iraqi Army, was a total success due to the generation of forces that were poised aboard

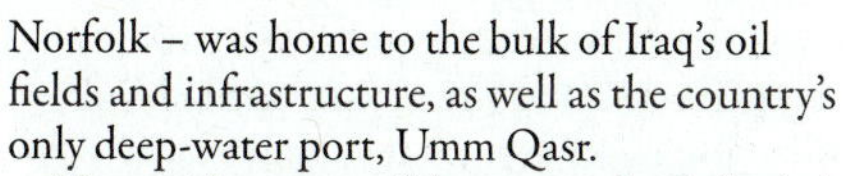

HMS *Ocean*. A helicopter assault, supported by hovercraft and landing craft quickly forced the Iraqi military in the area to collapse. The capture of the Al Faw peninsula deprived Saddam Hussein's regime of any oil revenue and prevented any attempt at a scorched earth policy, destroying the facilities and causing an ecological disaster, as occurred in Kuwait in 1991. Led by Brigadier Jim Dutton, the assault by 3 Commando Brigade which began on the night of March 20-21, 2003, with the attack on Al-Faw, involved more than 2,000 personnel, 80 helicopters, and successfully culminated just over a fortnight later with the fall of Iraq's second city of Basra.

Executed with determination and quiet professionalism, the operation led to substantial losses being inflicted on the enemy, hundreds of prisoners taken – including senior officers – key oil installations seized, aid shipments being delivered to Umm Qasr port, and the demoralisation of the Iraqi Army in the south of the country. The ARG had worked well but the advent of new technology, unmanned aerial drones, electronic warfare, and long-range weapons was to force the commandos to evolve further and meet new challenges in the 21st century.

The concept of large amphibious forces – which could be easy targets for modern weapons systems was to evolve again. Small 'bespoke' strike forces are the front edge of commando operations with the support ships ready to supplement them when the environment is safe. ●

The ARG had worked well but new technology, unmanned aerial drones and long-range weapons, was to force the commandos to evolve further and meet new challenges in the 21st century. (MOD)

AFGHANISTAN AND FUTURE OPERATIONS

Today's commando force has evolved to become a special maritime operations brigade capable of rapid intervention, hostage evacuation, and is poised to project military power with the deployment of small littoral strike groups. They operate in the high north and the Mediterranean and are ready to push east of Suez if required. In a new concept of operations termed the Future Commando Force, the marines are moving away from mass assaults across the beach and are focussed on small strike groups, capable of carrying out surveillance of a potential objective, advanced intervention to secure the evacuation of UK nationals, and supporting operations by other forces.

These small 'bespoke' forces be on called to deploy from their holding ships and navigate ashore using drones to identify threats as they advance towards the shore. New weapons, tactics and procedures have been and continue to be introduced as commanders 'test and adjust' the new order of battle. In the past, commandos deployed from assault ships – now submarines, helicopters, planes, and even ships hired from the commercial sector will be used to ferry the force into action. Drone and remote camera bots are being used to improve situational awareness when clearing buildings and on the battlefield. The days of infantry section attacks in the open will, as the war in Ukraine has demonstrated be limited in the future.

Britain's three main commando units have clearly assigned roles with 45 Commando dedicated to operations in the high north as the Littoral Strike Group North, as well as being on call for wider intervention missions. 40 Commando is the Littoral Strike Group South and deployed in the eastern Mediterranean and east of Suez while 42 Commando is the specialist maritime unit, with teams deployed aboard the fleet's aircraft carriers. They are ready to rescue fighter pilots if their aircraft go down in hostile areas and can field small teams in the Middle East ready to interdict arms and drugs smugglers. 47 Commando is a specialist force equipped with fast assault craft providing the maritime transport for the brigade while 30 Commando delivers the intelligence and surveillance requirements of the brigade. The current commando force structure comes after the brigade spent almost two decades in Afghanistan. As the force returned to contingency operations it was clear that technology had changed the shape of the battlespace – budgets were smaller, and HMS *Ocean* had been sold off.

Small 'bespoke' marine forces be on call to deploy from their holding ships and submarines - navigating ashore using drones to intercept potential threats. (MOD).

The UK's decision to deploy military force to Afghanistan followed the attack by al-Qaeda on the United States of America on September 11, 2001 and was part of a multi-national response. The aim was to stop the country, ravaged by decades of war, from remaining a 'safe haven' for terrorists. The plan was to stop the expansion of al-Qaeda and remove the Taliban from power in Kabul, by supporting the moderate Islamic Northern Alliance. The commandos were to be sent to Bagram airbase north of Kabul on a mission, Operation Jacanna, to support the US 10th Mountain Division and special forces as they hunted Osama bin Laden in the Tora Bora Mountains. That week, the Ministry of Defence announced that troops from 40 Commando RM, who had been on exercise in Oman, had deployed to Bagram Airfield, north of Kabul, which had been a strategic base for the Russians. The 40 Commando role was to provide 'force protection' and support for advance forces based at Bagram, the United States Army had deployed US Marines, US Special Forces, and the 10th Mountain Division to Bagram as part of Operation Enduring Freedom. The British offered to support them and in late 2001, the Ministry of Defence announced that 45 Commando RM, which was based in Scotland and trained in mountain warfare, would deploy in support of the Coalition in a new mission, codenamed Operation Jacanna.

The marines of 45 Commando RM were based at the top of the Bagram Airfield in a base named Camp Gibraltar after the Royal Marines' battle honour earned at 'the Rock' in 1704. During their searches of caves deep inside Tora Bora Mountains, the marines discovered hundreds of tons of explosives along with a considerable amount of other evidence of al-Qaeda's presence. Bin Laden himself, however, had gone. There was no sign and he had fled the area well beforehand. After months of operations in the mountains and on the Pakistan border, clearing caves used by the Taliban and al-Qaeda, and destroying stockpiles of abandoned weapons, 45 Commando RM had completed its task. Initially there had been a flurry of activity, but thereafter the marines became frustrated at the lack of direct combat against the Taliban or al-Qaeda. They adopted the Elvis Presley song *A Little Less Talk, A Little More Action* and played it constantly, but it failed to bring them the action they were ➲

Today's commando force has evolved to become a special maritime operations brigade capable of rapid intervention. (MOD)

The marines are moving away from mass assaults across the beach and are focussed on small strike groups which can be delivered into remote areas by helicopter, boat, and plane. (MOD)

45 Commando is dedicated to operations in the high north as the Littoral Strike Group North. (MOD)

anticipating so keenly. A political decision was now made made to withdraw 45 Cdo RM from Bagram by August 2002. Elements of 40 Cdo RM meanwhile remained on 'other' operations.

In September 2006, 3 Commando Brigade relieved 16 Air Assault Brigade in Helmand, southern Afghanistan. Here the commandos would operate with their colleagues in the US Marines, deploying into areas such as Garmsir and Nad-e-ali which would become common names. By late 2006 the deadly IED was now the Taliban's weapon of choice. In a move to counter the growing threat from roadside bombs, the commandos deployed with their Viking all terrain vehicles (ATV) that, although not fully armoured, provided an increased level of 'protected mobility'. In its role as the main strike force, 42 Cdo RM mounted a cycle of operations that involved each company deploying into the Gereshk Valley, followed by Now Zad, Kajaki, and Sangin. In December, M Company arrived at the base in Kajaki, now renamed FOB Zeebrugge. On New Year's Eve, the Marines had been briefed for a mission, codenamed Operation Clay, the following day. Insurgents had been observed around Kajaki and the marines' task was to clear them from the area. In the early hours, a force of some 110 marines and commando engineers moved into the area.

40 Commando is the Littoral Strike Group South and equipped with the latest technology. It deploys in the eastern Mediterranean and potentially east of Suez. (MOD)

As the company patrolled towards the compound of a known Taliban commander, 11 Troop was in the lead and came under attack. The marines quickly identified the location of the enemy and returned fire. As Corporal 'Jacko' Jackson led his section into the first compound to clear it they came under accurate fire from small arms and rocket propelled grenades (RPG, responding with 81mm mortars, heavy machine guns, and 84mm Interim Light Anti-Armour Weapons (ILAW). Once a foothold had been established within the compounds, 10 Troop were called forward to assist with the systematic clearing of the buildings. Several days later, on January 13, 2007, M Company found itself mounting another operation against the Taliban in Kajaki. During an assault into a compound, Marine Tom Curry,

In late 2001, the Ministry of Defence announced that 45 Commando RM, would deploy to Afghanistan in the hunt for Osama bin Laden – they quickly discovered huge weapons caches. (MOD)

The marines of 45 Commando found themselves high in the Tora Bora mountains and operating on the border with Pakistan amid concerns that bin Laden may skip across the border. (MOD)

42 Commando is the maritime specialist unit, with teams deployed aboard the fleet's aircraft carriers and small teams in the Middle East ready to interdict arms and drugs smugglers. (MOD)

A Royal Marine serving with 45 Commando pictured in a village high in the mountains near the Pakistan border on Operation Jacana. (MOD)

known as 'Vinders', was killed as the marines came under heavy fire. He was the first member of the UK Task Force to die in 2007.

Days earlier, on January 10, the Brigade Reconnaissance Force (BRF) – the intelligence 'eyes and ears' of the commander had been sent to Garmsir in the south of Helmand on a difficult and highly sensitive mission to confirm reports of a Taliban command post at Kosktay.

The target was deep south of Lashkar Gah and on the east side of the Helmand River, which required a river crossing that in winter would be a challenge. An initial attempt to cross in vehicles failed and thus the BRF opted to wade across instead. A reconnaissance to establish if this were possible was carried out in pitch darkness, with the temperature around minus 6°C, a small team waded half way across the

river, which was almost 100m wide in parts, and reported it could be done.

The operation was to be a raid and to be carried out by 24 members of the BRF who would strip off, pack their weapons, ammunition, and clothes in dry bags, hook on to a rope which tied them all together and wade across. The noise of the running water covering the crossing. Once across, the ➲

Mobile patrols from 45 Commando were deployed into wadis close to the Pakistan border and remained there for a week or more – being resupplied by helicopter. (DPL)

marines marched three kilometres to the target where they were to identify the Taliban target - a communications hub. Their commander, Captain Jason Milne, was in communication with a Nimrod MR-2 high above, but the aircraft's crew was unable to pinpoint the marines with their thermal cameras. Initially, they believed the marines were in the wrong place, but then realised that they were so cold from the crossing that they were not warm enough to give off a heat signature. The team's Joint Terminal Attack Controller (JTAC) radioed the exact grid reference of the target to a US Air Force (USAF) B-1 bomber en route to bomb the target. Once the bombs had been dropped, the marines stormed the building and secured all the useful information they found in the form of papers and photographs. The operation was a complete success and had been mounted in exactly the 'commando raid' style that young marines are taught in training.

On 11 December, 42 Commando conducted simultaneous helicopter and ground manoeuvre assaults on to the main objective of Nad e-Ali, to the northwest of Lashkar Gah. The enemy had fled, and the mission was a total success with the Commando now secure in compounds and with one company forming a 'block' to cut off routes for the enemy from the south. An immediate priority for the command group was to identify the local elders and inform them of the intention to bring security and stability to the area as well as road improvements.

With 42 Commando RM heavily engaged with the enemy in the north of the area of operations, the brigade commander Brigadier Thomas opted to 'force generate' a second battle group from resources he had at his disposal. The Information Exploitation (IX) Group had several units under command and

Forward operating bases were quickly secured in the border region of Afghanistan. The marines' vehicles were fitted with heavy machine guns and commandos carried extra ammunition and grenades. (MOD)

In December 2006, M Company 42 Commando, arrived at the base in Kajaki, now renamed FOB Zeebrugge and quickly prepared their orders for a mission named Operation Clay. (MOD)

In September 2006, 3 Commando Brigade deployed with their Viking all terrain vehicles (ATV) that, although not fully armoured, provided an increased level of 'protected mobility' – they were later replaced with a vehicle called the Warthog. (MOD)

On December 11, 2006, 42 Commando conducted simultaneous helicopter and ground manoeuvre assaults on to the main objective of Nad e-Ali, to the northwest of Lashkar Gah. (MOD)

was now given a much broader remit to take the fight to the enemy in the south at Garmsir. Sappers from 24 Cdo Regt RE moved in with plant and vehicles to upgrade roads and build two new patrol bases, but weather conditions were atrocious, and the heavy rain turned the area into a mud bath. K Company was tasked with disrupting the enemy and day after day fought in very difficult conditions over ground which resembled the Somme battlefield of the World War One.

On January 10, 2007, a warning order – a notice to all commandos within the unit of the pending operation - was issued and detailed the plan for an operation to raid a heavily fortified compound, known as Jugroom Fort. It was being used as a base for the Taliban to mount attacks in the area. The mission was planned to demonstrate that the Coalition was capable of operating anywhere it chose, psychologically disorientate the Taliban, and leave them on the defensive. The key objective was the Fort where a large number of enemy forces were known to be based, among them local commanders known to be active in Garmsir. It sat on a feature overlooking an expanse of desert, had high walls, and would be difficult to attack. To reach it, the marines would have to cross a river, then drive across open ground towards the objective in the Vikings that offered little protection from enemy fire. Prior to the assault a five-hour bombardment of artillery, mortars, B-1 bombers, F/A-18 Hornets, and AH-64 Apache attack helicopters would hit the fort hard and eliminate the enemy before Zulu Company dismounted and entered the complex. The commanding officer, Colonel Magowan had access to the Nimrod MR-2s' live imaging feed and planned for Zulu Company to strike just before dawn, kill any remaining insurgents, and destroy their equipment. When satisfied that they had accomplished their mission, the marines would withdraw back over the river and regroup at their assembly area. The mission was a success, but it quickly transpired that Lance Corporal Matthew Ford, of 5 Troop, was missing. Furthermore, it soon became apparent that he was still in the fort. All feared the worst that LCpl Ford had been taken prisoner, but no one said a word. A bold proposal was made to use two Apaches which

could lift four marines, two strapped to the outside of each aircraft, to the fort to retrieve the missing man and then fly them all out, the entire operation taking only a few minutes. Protection would be provided by two more Apaches loitering overhead. Col Magowan agreed to the plan and informed Brigadier Thomas. Four 'willing men' were quickly found. The Royal Marines were not prepared to leave a man behind. Sadly, LCpl Ford was discovered dead.

In late 2007, 40 Commando RM deployed to Helmand as part of 52 Infantry Brigade and faced an increased threat from roadside bombs and constant attacks. Marine Mark Ormrod, 24, lost both legs and his right arm and his colleague Ben McBean, 21, lost a leg and an arm. It was a violent tour and the unit lost three men during its six-month deployment - Lieutenant John Thornton, 23, Marine David Marsh, 22, and Corporal Damian Mulverhill.

In late 2008, 3 Commando Brigade were back in Helmand. A deliberate attack was planned and named as Operation Diesel. It was to involve 700 troops mounting an air assault, at night, deep into Taliban-held country. ⮑

The marines of 42 Commando found themselves in constant contact with the enemy, but their overwhelming firepower defeated the Taliban time and time again. (MOD)

Marines of 42 Commando's Lima Company fire support team lay down 7.62mm fire from a general-purpose machine gun. (MOD)

Two Army Air Corps AH-64 Apaches poured firepower into the Jugroom Fort prior to the marines' assault and then loitered in the area. (MOD)

the commando joined forces with the 3rd Battalion Royal Canadian Regiment (3 RCR) under command of the Canadian Task Force Kandahar and deployed to Zari Panjwayi, 20km south west of Kandahar.

In late 2009 while operating in the Sangin area, 40 Commando RM faced a ferocious month of fighting with ten marines killed and many injured. Captain Jonathan White, the commander of the unit's reconnaissance troop, was operating out of a patrol base next to the Chaka Shala Wadi, a Taliban stronghold. His father had been a Royal Marine and, having followed in his footsteps, Jonathan was commissioned at just 19 years old, which made him one of the youngest captains in the corps. Day after day the insurgents attacked the commandos as they tried to seize the town and gain influence in the area. Then, on June 16, Jonathan and his men deployed on a routine patrol in the

However, because 45 Cdo was committed to maintaining security across various bases, reinforcements were sought from 42 Cdo. Brigadier Gordon Messenger described Operation Diesel as a 'clinical precision strike' that had 'a powerful disruptive effect on known insurgent and narcotics networks in the area'. Four drugs' factories were captured along with chemicals used to process opium into heroin.

Meanwhile, 42 Commando RM, commanded by Lieutenant Colonel Charlie Strickland, was based in Kandahar and under command of the Dutch-commanded Regional Command South (RCS). As the force reserve, the unit was committed to operations across an area of operations from Zabul, Ursugan, Kandahar City, Helmand, and Nimruz. The unit's Lima Company had been the first 'on the ground' when 42 arrived in September, joining the Canadians and the Kandahar reconstruction team in a major clearance operation on September 22. In October,

For the rescue operation from the Jugroom Fort, a bold proposal was made to use two Apaches which could lift four marines, two strapped to the outside of each aircraft, to retrieve the missing man and then fly them all out, the entire operation taking only a matter of minutes. (MOD)

Prior to the assault on Jugroom Fort a five-hour bombardment of artillery, mortars, B-1 bombers, F/A-18 Hornets and WAH-64 Apache attack helicopters would hit the target hard and eliminate the enemy before the marines went in. (DPL)

The operation was regarded as a success, but the loss of LCpl Ford overshadowed the outcome. A service was later held to remember their lost colleague. (MOD)

Commando sharp shooters pictured in Helmand in 2010. (MOD)

In late 2008 the commandos mounted mobile operation groups throughout Afghanistan aimed at intercepting Taliban supply lines. (MOD)

the commandos returned to the UK and prepared to return to contingency operations it was quickly apparent that a new direction was needed.

A Changing Battlefield

While large assault ships and carriers had allowed the commandos to loiter in the ocean unseen, there was no hiding place in the 21st century with internet apps tracking ships and bloggers reporting anything and everything that moves. Drones, tactical camera bots, and computer algorithms were now being adopted to expose, compromise, and predict operational outcomes. The response was the Future Commando Force which will employ small littoral strike ships which can use electronic warfare to close down an adversary, deploy commandos by fast assault craft who protected by armed and navigational drones. These littoral plans will see one strike group of marines assigned to the high north while a second sits in the eastern Mediterranean with the potential to move east of Suez. Their role is to provide an 'on call' force to evacuate British nationals trapped in areas of civil unrest, assist in a hostage rescue or support humanitarian operations.

Traditional assault ships still have a role to deliver logistics and sustain a force, but modern weapons systems with long ranges prevent them from being in the frontline. The commandos see their new role as simply a response to the the future global threat. In one example of rapid intervention, marines from 40 Commando deployed to Sudan in April 2023 to help oversee the evacuation of British nationals trapped in Khartoum when fighting erupted between government and rebel forces. ●

dark hours of the early morning. They were on the edge of the area of operations as they monitored the landscape. He later recalled: "We had just stopped to remove our night-vision goggles and allow our eyes to adjust to the light, I remember moving uphill towards the man in front of me, the next thing I knew I was flying through the air and could only see the grey dawn sky. After 40 minutes I was loaded onto the MERT helicopter and, having not received any morphine, I screamed at the medics to put me to sleep, I woke three days later in the Queen Elizabeth Hospital at Selly Oak, and was discharged 27 days later."

In 2011 the commando brigade returned for their final tour with 42 and 45 Commando deployed in some of the most difficult regions of the province. As

In late 2008, 3 Commando Brigade were back in Helmand. A deliberate attack was planned and named as Operation Diesel. It was to involve 700 troops mounting an air assault at night. (MOD)

COMMANDOS IN 2045

The Commando Force of 2045 and beyond will be fully supported by digital technology and capable of delivering greater effect with smaller forces; adopting autonomous technology which can be integrated into the force. These unmanned platforms can provide medical evacuation, surveillance, air defence, and direct mobile firepower generated from wheeled and tracked vehicles, as well as operating in the sub-surface and airborne environment. Commandos will no longer be able guarantee technical superiority on the battlefield as non-state actors, who increasingly act as proxy forces for regional powers, are heavily armed with modern weapons. It will become increasingly difficult to move and hide as enemy sensors and surveillance systems become more powerful.

The war in Ukraine has demonstrated that the battlefield can be penetrated and controlled by technology as drones fitted with heat seeking cameras hunt down soldiers and

Future commando operations will remain centred around the littoral and will increasingly focus on the use of technology. (MOD)

Commandos will benefit from situational awareness technology in which drones will transmit aerial images and maps to a tablet worn on the soldiers' chest. (MOD)

weakness. The world will be a very different place in 2045 and defence scientists predict that robots and artificial technology will dominate the battlefield with some experts stating that the pace of future intelligence systems will allow commanders to use their thoughts to engage weapon systems. It seems a remote concept, but neurotechnologies can enable this to happen. There are already some examples of such futuristic innovations in action, like brain implants controlling prosthetic arms. By 2045 we can expect to see an increase in population of three billion, scarcity of resources, increased vulnerability of overpopulated cities, and more inequality – all pinch points for conflict.

Environmental Attacks

A study published by the UK Ministry of Defence in 2014 claimed that in future we could experience a sophisticated environmental attack, capable of spreading plant and human diseases by insects or insect-machine hybrids. Conspiracy theorists claim the pandemic was generated in the Far East to undermine Western economies and to test Western readiness for an eco-war. While there is little evidence that this is what happened, the ability to spread

disease remains a significant threat. The report also listed a war between the US and China as just one of the potentially devastating future scenarios. It claimed that drones will become cheaper to manufacture and fall into the wrong hands – a situation that has already happened.

To meet future requirements, the commandos are generating a balanced force which will include female soldiers and train both men and women to operate a range of highly sophisticated weapons and equipment. The force of 2045 will continue to focus on the littoral – the coastline – with Royal Marine Commandos deployed aboard littoral strike ships to provide a global military presence. By 2045 new ships, designed with a lower profile to evade radar, are due to enter service. They will carry support helicopters and fast attack craft as well as autonomous boats which can be used for surveillance and target acquisition. These ships will embrace the latest technology with an operations room that will allow commanders to deploy robots ashore as part of an advanced reconnaissance force prior to sending in a commando strike force. An electronic shield will protect the commando force and prevent an adversary

deliver their position to artillery units or an armed drone team. In 2045, weapons will have the ability to kill with greater range and accuracy. Adversaries will continue to adopt an asymmetric approach in an attempt to bypass the commandos' combat strength and find a

Fast strike craft will ferry commandos ashore using drones to identify threats (MOD)

Helicopters are expected to remain in service for another 20 years but could be augmented by revolutionary new methods of delivery from future ships. (MOD)

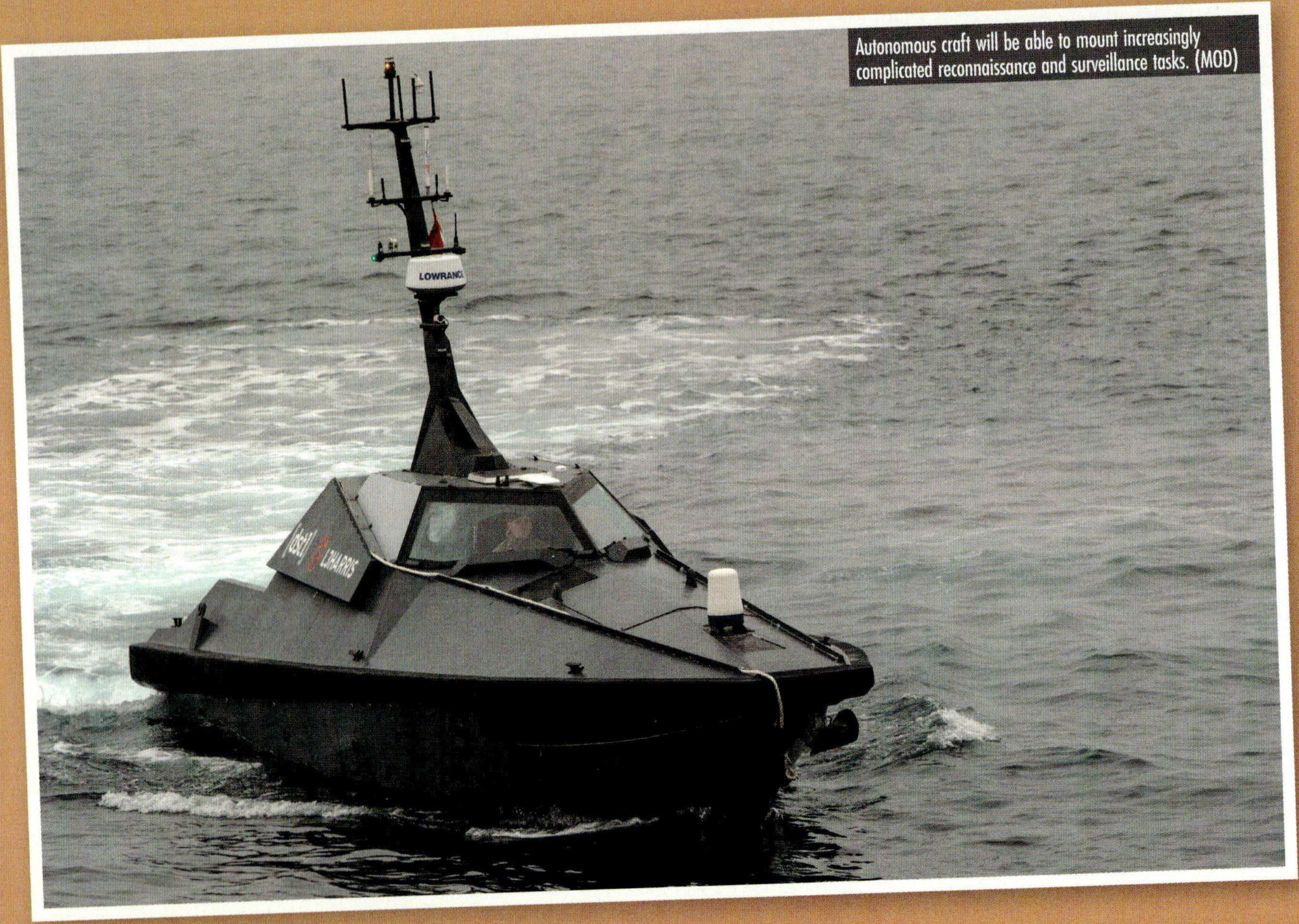

Autonomous craft will be able to mount increasingly complicated reconnaissance and surveillance tasks. (MOD)

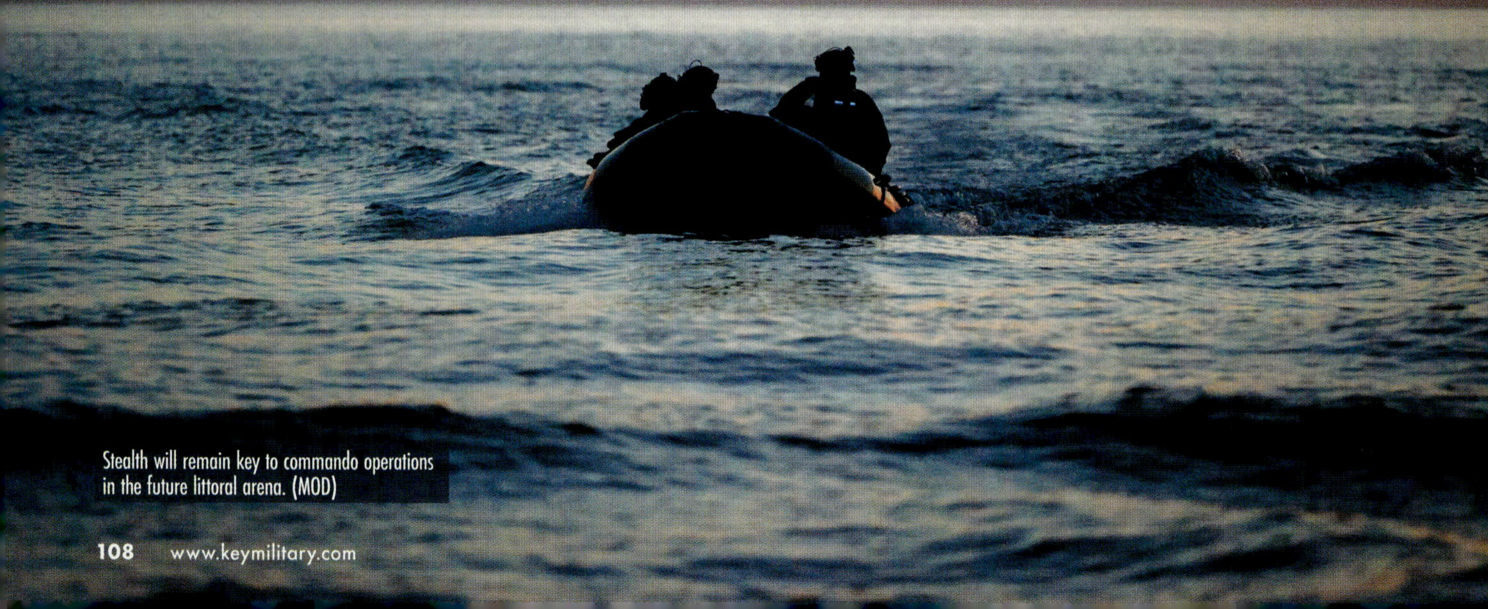

from mounting a network attack. The littoral ships will be supported by direct energy weapons (lasers) which will be fitted to all future Royal Navy ships. In a future conflict the commandos could find themselves operating in contested waters where enemy forces have long range weapons and deploy 'access denial' measures in the form of electronic counter measures, remote activated mines, and robot defences. To counter this threat, military scientists are developing systems to ensure the Littoral Strike Group (LSG) maritime shipping will be protected. These will include systems such as the new DragonFire laser which can neutralise airborne threats such as drones, missiles, and enemy aircraft. In addition, if when the green berets go ashore, they come under sustained attack, DragonFire can be used to protect the force. Its precision allows it to hit a target the size of a £1 coin from a kilometre away reducing collateral damage and civilian casualties.

Being ready for 2045 and beyond means being ahead of potential adversaries, many of whom adopt tactics which ignore the international guidelines listed in the law of armed conflict. The commandos are embracing technology to develop innovative approaches to warfare which include using small 'robots' fitted with a camera which can be thrown into a building or room and provide the strike team with a live feed of activity within the target room.

Areas of Interest

At present the commandos' two Littoral Strike Groups (LSG) are established aboard naval support vessels - often Bay class ships. Both groups are assigned to specialist areas - the High North off Norway, Sweden, and Finland with a second LSG being deployed into the Mediterranean and east of Suez. The LRG(North) is focused on the reinforcement of NATO's northern flank and the threat of a Russian incursion, while the LRG(South) maintains a footprint in the Middle East in response to threats against UK interests and the protection of British citizens working and living in the region. The commandos' mission in 2045 will continue to focus on what politicians

Stealth will remain key to commando operations in the future littoral arena. (MOD)

Operations in the high north will remain a priority in support of NATO. (MOD)

and military chiefs' call 'areas of interest' (AOI). These are regions where the UK has significant trade interests and in some cases commonwealth obligations as well as security concerns. Other AOIs include former British colonies who remain closely linked to the UK through trade or political agreement and may seek military support, such as in the case of the Sierra Leone government who called on London for assistance when rebels threaten to overthrow the capital Freetown in 2000.

Countries on the verge of conflict are also of interest as British citizens may be in danger and need evacuating. In the next two decades the impact of climate change in Africa is likely to act as a catalyst for more conflict as countries face water shortages and famine. The priority AOIs will remain the international shipping lanes in the Red Sea and the South China Sea which are vital to both British and European trade.

In the Middle East, Iran frequently makes claim to the sovereignty of the Strait of Hormuz waterway – the vital transit route to Bahrain. Here commandos currently mount a permanent

Marine commandos intercepted an Iranian tanker off Gibraltar in 2019 demonstrating their capability to intercept vessels on the high seas. (MOD)

maritime counterterrorist presence which analysts expect to continue. In nearby Yemen the Houthis, a proxy militia funded and armed by Iran, have attempted to close the Red Sea by attacking merchant shipping in support of Palestinians in Gaza. This international waterway is the gateway to and from the Suez Canal and is expected to be a future 'pinch point' where the commandos will be deployed.

Elsewhere, China is expected to continue its political aspiration to dominate trade in the Pacific while maintaining its sovereignty claims over Taiwan and much of the South China Seas. This has resulted in the UK forming a military partnership with Australia to protect trade interests and in March 2024 the LSG(South) deployed for manoeuvres in Darwin with marines from 40 Commando embarked on the support ships RFA *Lyme Bay* and *Argus*.

Future threats facing the commando force in the next two decades will most likely, be driven by the same factors that have historically prompted conflict: sovereignty claims, protection of resources, trade, and ➲

The demands of the Arctic will continue to require a high level of combat training. (MOD)

In 2023 the first signs of the use of artificial Intelligence for military purposes was seen in the Sudan civil war when rebel forces posted 'cloned' interviews of the former President to influence the community. (Sudan Government)

Drones are increasingly being used in all areas of military operations and are embedded in commando missions. (MOD)

economic disparities as well as the pursuit of power and influence. But the battlespace in which war is waged will change as artificial intelligence (AI) emerges and more state and non-state actors gain access to these capabilities. AI can be implemented across the force from planning, deception, and the actual execution of the mission. From warfare systems, to target recognition, cyber security and the drone swarms, AI systems can be used to inform decisions about who or what to attack and when. The most significant development in AI has been the wide public availability of generative AI which has seen the improvement in language creation with applications such as ChatGPT. Other programmes allow total manipulation of an incident or conversation to influence an audience.

Warfare systems carried by the commando force such as weapons, sensors, navigation,

Landing craft or helicopters can deliver light autonomous vehicles ashore which can be used as direct fire platforms or to evacuate wounded soldiers. (MOD)

aviation support, and surveillance equipment can employ AI in order to make operations more efficient and less reliant on human input. This additional efficiency means that these systems may require less maintenance. AI will allow a commando strike team to launch and control multiple drones in a 'swarm attack'. These Unmanned Aerial Platforms (UAVs) can launch a computer network attack to close down an enemy communications system, create a deception as part of an influence operation or mount a direct attack. AI has the obvious capability of informing and influencing and was used in the 2023 civil war in Sudan.

In 2019, Omar al-Bashir, the former President of Sudan, had been toppled by the military after allegations of war crimes and fraud. Then in 2023 a rebel militia known as the Rapid Support Force launched an operation to seize power. During the conflict, an anonymous 'fake' account was posted online in which the voice of the former President had been cloned in 'leaked recordings' which indicated that Bashir had been involved in launching the attacks against government forces. The recording received thousands of views on social media. In further

Technology is now allowing commandos to control up to 20 drones which can map a battlefield or mount a swarm operation. (MOD)

Autonomous platforms can work in tandem with drones providing air cover for ground-based platforms. (MOD)

Small 'bots' fitted with cameras can easily be carried by commandos and thrown into rooms to provide a visual picture of the space before soldiers enter. (MOD)

examples of AI-generated fake content, film was distributed showing government fighter aircraft flying low and fast over the airport which some international news companies used believing it to be real. Prior to 40 Commando arriving at Khartoum to evacuate British nationals, pictures had been posted online suggesting the airfield had been bombed. It hadn't, and the images were fake. Campaigns like this are significant and in future will be used to disorientate and dislocate enemy forces.

Future Now

In 2023 the commandos' future tactics are already being seen: small maritime strike teams are going ashore with a drone above them allowing them to identity threats, while using an electronic jamming capability to close down networks in the area they are approaching. In the future they will use hand held phones which can transmit secure speech from the Far East to the UK – without leaving any digital footprint for an adversary to track and trace. Robotic and autonomous vehicles will become common. As the strike force approaches the shore a robot force will be the first to step onto dry land. Sub-surface platforms will be employed to search the shoreline for obstacles and mines before the signal is given to start a raid. ➲

Often called Unmanned Ground Vehicles, these small, tracked platforms can be used for surveillance. (MOD)

Future planning will be configured around digital maps and live video feeds onto large screens. (MOD)

The Royal Marine Commandos have been issued with light, all-terrain vehicles which can be driven into and out of the back of a helicopter. (MOD)

Small and highly mobile, these four-man vehicles can be airlifted or driven into the back of a Chinook helicopter. (MOD)

An autonomous platform fitted with a heavy machine gun. (MOD)

The commandos will wear special uniforms which will hide the heat of their bodies and protect them from thermal imaging cameras and drones. A mission to rescue a hostage will see a robot team deployed to mount a deception and contain an enemy force while the human commandos raid the target and rescue the captive. Night-vision systems have been in service for some time , but new systems which incorporate thermal imagery – to detect heat from a body - and peripheral proximity alerts which sense movement either side of the soldier will be introduced into service.

New equipment will provide situational awareness and allow a commando to view the battlefield around him or her on a small chest-mounted screen. Autonomous vehicles will include an Unmanned Ground Vehicle or UGV which can support surveillance operations. Despite its small size it would not be used by the strike team and instead would be deployed by the deception force relaying information to the command team on the littoral strike ship and the assault force. Other unmanned platforms include the Robotic Platoon Vehicle (RPV) which would need to be launched by a landing craft as part of a follow-on force. It can be fitted with a heavy machine gun and used to advance on the flanks of the astride force. As the commando force shapes itself for the future, new weapons such as the KS01 assault rifle are being introduced. It features advanced optical and thermal sights as well as a suppressor for stealth. The future plan for the commando force will see them operating increasingly with the US Marines in a role that will see them continue to be ready for operations from the Arctic to the desert.

To ensure they are ready for 2045, the Royal Marines are investigating future capabilities – including launching commandos ashore from an electro-magnetic rail gun mounted on a Royal Navy ship in Sycamore Stealth Pods which enter high altitudes at high supersonic speeds giving them ranges of more than 100 miles. These bullet shaped projectiles ➲

An artist's impression of the potential new Littoral Strike Ships (MOD)

Drones are being used to resupply commandos with ammunition and logistics support. (MOD)

are not intended as munitions, they can carry supplies and are large enough even to fit a Royal Marine Commando. Two sets of contra-rotating blades open during the pod's descent, bringing them to earth quietly for covert insertions. The rotating blades power a generator, with the energy generated being stored to act as a power source. Ekranoplans – stealth vehicles which can deliver the commandos and may replace the littoral strike ships – are also being investigated. These sleek, narrow, low drag platforms will be able to reach speeds of 100kts and incorporate active camouflage to enhance stealth capability. Laser guns and special gloves with electric pulse which allow cliff assault teams to hold onto any surface are being explored along with helmets that deliver battlefield information to each member of the team.

All this equipment will take time to develop and bring to service. It should improve a commando's over the horizon vision and their awareness of the near battlefield enemy – but in the meantime, the force remains committed to using what it terms the 'mark one eyeball'. ●

Arriving in the dead of night from the sea - a tactic the commandos have embraced since their formation in World War Two. (MOD)